JOURNEYMAN ELECTRICIAN
EXAM PREP 2023 - 2024

MASTER THE EXAM WITH THIS STUDY GUIDE & PASS IT EFFORTLESSLY ON THE FIRST TRY | GET TOP SCORES THANKS TO THE SIMPLE EXPLANATIONS & TIPS OF AN EXPERT TRAINER

EDITION 2023-2024

CONNOR BENNETT

JOURNEYMAN ELECTRICIAN EXAM PREP 2023-2024
Master the Exam with This Study Guide & Pass It Effortlessly on the First Try | Get Top Scores with the Simple Explanations & Tips of an Expert Trainer

First Edition July 2023

© **Copyright 2023 by Carter J. Bennett - All rights reserved.**

This document is geared towards providing exact and reliable information regarding the topic and issue covered. The publication is sold with the idea that the publisher is not required to render accounting, officially permitted, or otherwise qualified services. If advice is necessary, legal, or professional, a practiced individual in the profession should be ordered.

- From a Declaration of Principles, which was accepted and approved equally by a Committee of the American Bar Association and a Committee of Publishers and Associations.

In no way is it legal to reproduce, duplicate, or transmit any part of this document in either electronic means or in printed format. Recording of this publication is strictly prohibited, and any storage of this document is not allowed unless with written permission from the publisher. All rights reserved.

The information provided herein is stated to be truthful and consistent in that any liability, in terms of inattention or otherwise, by any usage or abuse of any policies, processes, or directions contained within is the solitary and utter responsibility of the recipient reader. Under no circumstances will any legal responsibility or blame be held against the publisher for any reparation, damages, or monetary loss due to the information herein, either directly or indirectly.

Respective authors own all copyrights not held by the publisher.

The information herein is offered for informational purposes solely and is universal as so. The presentation of the information is without a contract or any type of guarantee assurance.

The trademarks that are used are without any consent, and the publication of the trademark is without permission or backing by the trademark owner. All trademarks and brands within this book are for clarifying purposes only and are owned by the owners themselves, not affiliated with this document.

This document is geared towards providing exact and reliable information regarding the topic and issue covered. The publication is sold with the idea that the publisher is not required to render accounting, officially permitted, or otherwise, qualified services. If advice is necessary, legal, or professional, a practiced individual in the profession should be ordered.

- From a Declaration of Principles, which was accepted and approved equally by a Committee of the American Bar Association and a Committee of Publishers and Associations. In no way is it legal to reproduce, duplicate, or transmit any part of this document in either electronic means or in printed format. Recording of this publication is strictly prohibited, and any storage of this document is not allowed unless with written permission from the publisher. All rights reserved. The information provided herein is stated to be truthful and consistent, in that any liability, in terms of inattention or otherwise, by any usage or abuse of any policies, processes, or directions contained within is the solitary and utter responsibility of the recipient reader. Under no circumstances will any legal responsibility or blame be held against the publisher for any reparation, damages, or monetary loss due to the information herein, either directly or indirectly. Respective authors own all copyrights not held by the publisher. The information herein is offered for informational purposes solely and is universal as so. The presentation of the information is without a contract or any type of guarantee assurance. The trademarks that are used are without any consent, and the publication of the trademark is without permission or backing by the trademark owner. All trademarks and brands within this book are for clarifying purposes only and are owned by the owners themselves, not affiliated with this document.

JOURNEYMAN ELECTRICIAN EXAM PREP 2023-2024

Master the Exam with This Study Guide & Pass It Effortlessly on the First Try | Get Top Scores with the Simple Explanations & Tips of an Expert Trainer

CONNOR BENNETT

TABLE OF CONTENTS

INTRODUCTION 7

CHAPTER 1
JOURNEYMAN ELECTRICIAN EXAM GUIDE 11
1.1 Exam for Journeyman Electricians 12

CHAPTER 2
NATIONAL ELECTRIC CODE 19
2.1 History of NEC 20
2.2 The National Electrical Code's Application 20
2.3 Importance of NEC's Enforcement for Ensuring Workplace Safety 20
2.4 NEC Adoption in Electrical Installations 21
2.5 Structure of NEC 21

CHAPTER 3
ELECTRIC SAFETY MEASURES 23
3.1 Common Safety Measures 24
3.2 Electricians: Workplace Safety Guidance 26

CHAPTER 4
BASICS OF ELECTRICAL THEORY 31
4.1 Learning Fundamental Electrical Theory 32
4.2 What Is a Switch? 35
4.3 Branch Circuits 36
4.4 Electric Circuit 39
4.5 What Is Feeder? 45

CHAPTER 5
ELECTRICAL WIRING SYSTEM 49
5.1 Electrical Wiring 50
5.2 Electrical Wiring Procedures 50
5.3 Electrical Wiring System Types 51

5.4 Grounding of Electrical Systems 53
5.5 Electrical Boxes 54
5.6 Electrical Raceways 55

CHAPTER 6
TRANSFORMERS AND ELECTRIC MOTORS 59
6.1 Transformer 60
6.2 Working Principal of a Transformer 60
5.3 .....Types of Transformers..61
6.4 Electric Motors 64
6.5 Types of Electric Motors 64
6.6 Starting Method of Induction Motor 67
6.7 Slip Ring Starter Method 68
6.8 Maintenance of the Electric Motor 68
6.9 Electric Motor Protection Devices 70

CHAPTER 7
CONTROL AND LIGHTING SYSTEM 71
7.1 Control System...72
7.2 Lighting System 75
7.3 The Lighting System's Design 75
7.4 The Lighting System Management 75
7.5 Types of Lighting 76

CHAPTER 8
ELECTRICAL GROUNDING 79
8.1 Electrical Grounding 80

CHAPTER 9
ELECTRICAL DRAWING 83
9.1 Electrical Drawing 84

CHAPTER 10
ELECTRICAL EQUIPMENT AND TOOLS 89
10.1 Electrical Tools 90
10.2 Hand Tools 90
10.3 Power Tools..92
10.4 Electrician Safety Equipment 94
10.5 Other Electrical Safety Devices 95

CHAPTER 11
ELECTRICAL MAINTENANCE AND TROUBLESHOOTING 97
11.1 What is Troubleshooting? 98
11.2 What Causes Electrical Equipment Failures? 98
11.3 Techniques for Troubleshooting Electrical Equipment 99
11.4 Hardware Troubleshooting Tools Electricians Need................................101
11.5 Troubleshooting and Maintenance of Advanced Electrical Equipment and Systems 101

CHAPTER 12
CONDUIT BENDING AND INSTALLATION..105
12.1 Electrical Conduit...106
12.2 What Materials Are Used to Make Conduit Bodies? 106
12.3 Types of Electrical Conduits 106

CHAPTER 13
PRACTICE TEST 113
Practice Test 1 114
Practice Test 2 117
Practice Test 3 119
Practice Test 4 122
Practice test 5 125
Practice Test 6 128
Practice Test 7 131
Practice Test 8 134
Practice Test 9 138
Practice Test 10 141

GLOSSARY OF TERMINOLOGY 145

CONCLUSION 148

INTRODUCTION

Those who have finished a sizable percentage of the education necessary to become licensed electricians are known as Journeyman Electricians. Becoming a certified electrician is their ultimate professional goal. These individuals build and repair electrical connections and infrastructure for homes, workplaces, and commercial buildings.

They will undertake examinations of the connections, transformers, and circuit breakers as part of their duties. To ensure that all the electrical work finished on a project complies with those rules and regulations, they will also need to be conversant with the rules established in the code for construction. To make sure that the structure is built correctly and positioned in the proper spot, they also need to understand blueprints.

10% of electricians work on their own, based on statistics gathered by the US Bureau of Labor Statistics in 2014. Although some prefer to continue their formal study at a Technology College, apprenticeship is still the conventional instruction route for electricians.

What does "journeyman electrician" entail?

Having the necessary knowledge to function independently in one's field of study without having the degree of license needed to work as a professional electrician is what it means to be a journeyman electrician. They may be required to operate on peripherals such as powering hydraulic systems and permanent devices in businesses, factories, and residential facilities. However, working on an institution's power and electricity system for the first time is typically not the job of journeyman electricians. Only licensed expert electricians can handle this work.

If you were a journeyman electrician, you might have connected switches, circuit breakers, transformers, and outlets. Other responsibilities can involve setting up lighting and security measures. Along with overseeing trainees' work, you may also inspect and evaluate the dependability of the current wiring systems.

What type of knowledge will I require?

After four years, students who complete the training program are normally eligible for career employment and licensing. One of these programs is often how an electrician learns their trade. Trade associations and labor unions like the International Brotherhood of Electrical Workers and the International Electrical Contractors provide financial support for these. It's possible that community organizations and technical schools also provide apprenticeship programs.

Throughout the program's lecture portion, you will receive over 600 hours of tutorials regarding electricity theories, analyzing blueprints, and learning the electric code's needs and rules. Additionally, you will be trained while working for a total of 8000 hours. You can be requested to perform various tasks, such as installing stakes, boring holes, and connecting and testing wires. An expert electrician supervises your task the entire time.

Do I require a license to drive?

Although the requirements differ from state to state, in most cases, you must possess eight thousand hours of work experience skills or a minimum of four to five years of necessary employment experience to complete this procedure. Several jurisdictions require certification or licensing for journeymen electricians. You can also be required to do well on a written exam covering the National Electrical Code (NEC), the local electrical code, and electrical theory.

Additionally, each state has its unique standards for examining licenses or certifications. In some jurisdictions, you might need to participate in ongoing educational events and accumulate credits to keep your electrician qualification. Further learning is mandated in some areas but not in others.

By using the suggestions and techniques in this book, readers will be well-prepared for this difficult yet fulfilling career. In this book, you can succeed and advance your career with perseverance, commitment, and knowledge. This practical guide to preparing for the Electrician Certification Exam is an extensive guide that offers readers the details they need to pass the certification test and become licensed electricians.

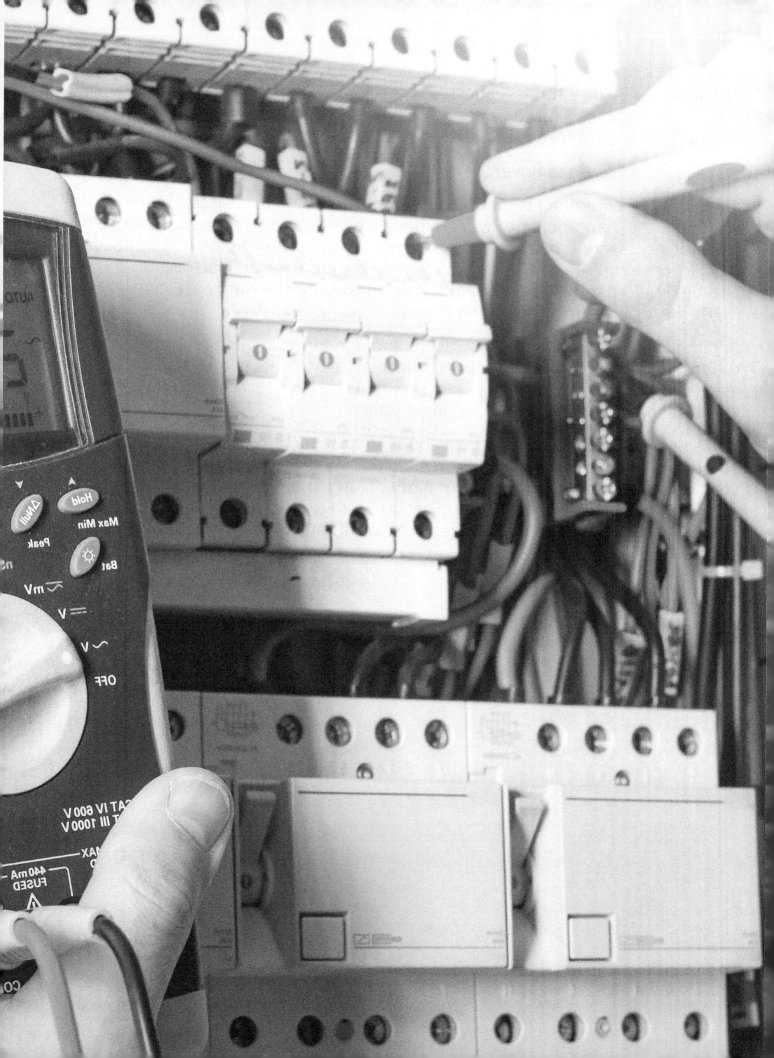

CHAPTER 1
JOURNEYMAN ELECTRICIAN EXAM GUIDE

Each state has strict regulations governing electricians' work to protect the public. Most states require electricians to hold a license as a matter of law. In many states, obtaining a license requires passing an exam. Licensed master electricians and electrical contractors may direct licensed journeyman electricians to operate unattended on a job site.

1.1 Exam for Journeyman Electricians

This test is designed to ascertain whether a candidate possesses the relevant expertise and knowledge to be licensed as a general electrician. State-to-state variations in exam style and subject matter generally test candidates' understanding of fundamental electrical theory and the electrical code. Entry-level knowledge of low-voltage systems and wiring in residential, commercial, and other environments is typically expected of a journeyman electrician. The licensing tests frequently cover the following topics:

- Electrical terminology
- Equipment and services for electricity
- Feeders for electricity
- Conductors of branch circuits
- Techniques for electrical wiring
- Electrical components
- Generators and motors
- Electrical switchboards and disconnectors
- Technology for renewable energy

Before they may take the licensing exam, most jurisdictions that require electricians to be licensed also demand that they have a high school diploma or GED and have finished a 3–5-year apprenticeship program with a master or journeyman electrician. Some employers and unions may also require electricians to obtain an associate degree.

Regional building departments give the licensing test for electricians. Get in touch with your neighborhood building department to register for the test. Request a copy of the exam's blueprint from the building department. This blueprint will tell you how many and what kind of questions are on the test and how much time you have to finish it. You might find out from the blueprint the required grade to pass the test. The National Electrical Code Book may be used where stated in exams' open and closed book sections. The usage of tabbed NEC books is permitted in several areas.

Common locations for the journeyman electrician tests include local government buildings or community institutions. Once you are eligible, register for the exam.

Applicants are advised to read this complete handbook to ensure they understand the exam procedure and governing laws.

1. General Points

The National Electrical Code (NEC) or National Electrical Safety Code is available without tabs or other help in soft-cover form. The National Electrical Code edition used for the exam is the one that has been incorporated into the state's construction code. The most recent edition of the National Electrical Safety Code is used when the test is given. The Laws and Rules Booklet offered for the exam is in the current layout. The Department uses and contains the laws and regulations in force when the test is given.

- The instructions for the exam should be comprehensive, clear, and easy to understand. The test administrator (examination moderator) cannot be questioned.
- The examination room may be electronically monitored and watched over by the on-site proctor.
- Applicants must understand the question without having to read the possible responses.
- Candidates taking an exam may leave the room to use the bathroom, but they cannot leave the building. Application failure, the need to reapply, and payment of the necessary costs will result in applicants departing the facility before finishing their examination.
- The knowledge domains covered under the applicable license are the subject of the exam questions.
- Applicants caught duplicating questions or taking notes will be automatically rejected and forced to submit a fresh application along with the necessary expenses.
- The exam questions reasonably cover the knowledge domains within the purview of the relevant license.
- Applications seen offering or receiving assistance from other candidates or third parties will be instantly rejected, and fresh applications must be submitted with the necessary costs.
- Common knowledge domains are referenced in exam questions. The exam knowledge domains fall within the categories of employment that people applying for or having the relevant license class typically encounter.
- Candidates are permitted to utilize an electronic calculator, a Laws and Rules Booklet, the National Electrical Code, or the National Electrical Safety Code (used only for the lineman exam) throughout the test. No code references are nec-

essary as part of any solution unless expressly stated otherwise by a specific question. The Department supplies a calculator and all reference materials. No additional items or electronics, including cell phones, are permitted inside the structure. Even though reference materials are available during the entire exam, candidates should come prepared and not rely solely on the materials to answer all questions. The vast majority of questions are designed to be answered by the applicant without the requirement for a reference source.

2. Format of Questions

The format of the questions in the Journeyman Electrician test is as follows:

- The format of the exam questions requires the applicant to show that they have a thorough understanding of the subject matter.
- Questions with variables ensure that the right knowledge domain(s) or coding rule(s) must be used to arrive at the right response.
- The wording of the multiple-choice answers for knowledge areas with numerous conditions or requirements is chosen to minimize the applicant's potential to choose the right answer(s) based on keywords and demand that the applicant demonstrate knowledge of the subject matter.
- Negative-response questions, such as "Which of the following does NOT apply," are only occasionally employed. The multiple-correct response format mentioned in item 3 above has a companion format.
- Selecting the incorrect multiple-choice response is "plausible."
- Extraneous information may be included in questions.
- Unless otherwise specified in individual questions, the power factor for all questions and corresponding answers is assumed to be "unity."
- A few queries concern persistent code violations committed by electrical wire installers. To guarantee the applicant has a thorough and correct understanding of electrical theory and code, excellent instruction must be supplemented by practical experience.

3. Format of Examination

The journeyman examination for an electrician is the Open Codebook examination. The duration of the exam is 2 hours and 30 minutes. There are 80 multiple-choice questions in the exam. Each question is worth 1.25 points.

The first part of the journeyman exam involves Fundamentals and Practical Electricity. In this part, there are 20 questions for a total of 25 points. Part 8 Rules are involved in the second part of the exam. In the second part, there are 10 questions for

12.5 points total. In the third part of the exam, 50 questions related to the National Electric Code total 62.5 points. In this way, the total points for the exam are 100.

4. Result of Examination

- Applicants receive email and mail notification of their exam results within two weeks. Applicants are not given telephone access to exam results.
- Instructions on how to submit a subsequent application are included in the examination result letters sent to applicants who did not pass their exams.
- Instructions on how to obtain a license are included in the examination result letters sent to applicants who completed their exams.

5. Exam Revision or Appeal

- Exams are rechecked to guarantee correctness when results are within five (5) percentage points of passing.
- Candidates who are unsuccessful on any exam may apply to retake it 30 days after receiving news that they failed.
- Candidates cannot request oral or written evaluations of their tests. Candidates may submit written feedback on particular exam questions to the department's licensing section.

6. Strategies and Tips to Pass Journeyman Electrician's Exam

It can be difficult to prepare for the Journeyman Electrician's Exam. It takes effort, patience, and time. To achieve this, students must exhibit self-motivation. It could be a little more difficult, but it is still feasible! There are methods to deal with this new reality and emerge from it stronger. The following study advice will help you pass the Journeyman Electrician's Exam.

I. Read the Text All the Way Through

Complete a thorough reading of the material while you are starting so that you can begin to understand the information. Giving yourself a solid foundation to build on is crucial for success because repetition is essential for learning.

II. Investigate Test Preparation Options

Research extra study resources such as books, apps, test preparation classes, and other tools.

III. Take Notes by Hand

According to studies, taking well-organized handwritten notes facilitates learning. Because you prefer to organize knowledge into more practical forms when taking handwritten notes, they have been demonstrated to be more productive. It creates a greater sense of knowledge and more intense mental engagement.

IV. Do Not Study While You Are Sleep Deprived

Your brain may learn that studying while fatigued is equivalent to taking a nap. You're more prone to experience exam fatigue if you study while exhausted. Make sure you get plenty of sleep and study when you're awake.

V. Prepare a "Cheat Sheet" or Study Guide With the Concepts You Need to Review!

Preparing a study guide or "cheat sheet" enables you to connect ideas, identify trends, and keep track of the material you still need to review. A study guide will serve as a direction for your future study and increase the effectiveness and efficiency of the learning process.

VI. When in Doubt, Seek Assistance

If you don't know the solution, don't give up! Never hesitate to ask for assistance from your lecturers, fellow students, or even your boss! Try an internet forum or get advice from a professional in your industry if you can't figure out the solution or don't understand why something is the correct response.

VII. Give Topics that You Don't Understand as Much Priority

Humans may want to learn things we already understand to make ourselves feel better. Spend a large amount of time acquiring new concepts or refining ones you don't comprehend if you want to succeed. If you don't know anything right away, don't give up! Instead, focus and make a sincere effort to study it!

i. Set a Target

Setting daily goals for your study time will keep you on track, hold you accountable, and stop procrastination. For instance, to ensure that you are actively progressing in your learning, establish a target of studying 25 questions today.

VIII. Keep Your Study Area Organized and Tidy

It's crucial to be calm and undistracted while studying. Remember, a clean environment promotes a clear mind.

IX. Follow the 50/10 Rule

According to the 50/10 rule, you should study for 50 minutes before taking a 10-minute break. This keeps your mind active and avoids mental fatigue. Always stretch and maintain proper posture.

X. Attempt to Minimize Interruptions

Home study can be challenging. To maximize your study time, try to be attentive and involved in what you are doing. Distractions from the visual and aural world can prevent you from learning. Close the door, mute your phone, and think about inserting earplugs.

XI. Link Notions and Theories to Actual Experiences

Your awareness and comprehension of the theory or concept are solidified when you can relate it to real-world applications. It enhances memory and can increase productivity in your study and professional lives. Try to relate what you learn in class to your everyday tasks at work, for instance, if you are an apprentice at a construction site.

XII. Create a Test Environment Simulation

Simulating the testing atmosphere is crucial when studying for or taking a practice test. Make sure to take several complete practice exams to prepare for the test.

XIII. Test Yourself or Allow Someone Else to Do So

By testing your knowledge and increasing repetition, quizzes let you assess what you have learned. You can then decide what needs to be improved and move forward from there.

XIV. Use Practice Exams

Practice tests allow you to test your knowledge and understanding like quizzes, providing a true reflection of your knowledge.

CHAPTER 2
NATIONAL ELECTRIC CODE

The National Fire Protection Association, an American safety organization, published the National Electrical Code guidelines as a safety standard. In residential, commercial, and industrial buildings, the NEC serves as a collection of model requirements for the secure installation of electrical equipment or any kind of electrical installation.

Since the NFPA is not a government agency, the NEC lacks any inherent legal significance. However, each version of the NEC is written in legalese to make it simple for its provisions to become legislation. The NEC has been enacted into law by numerous Latin American countries, all 50 states, and at the regional level.

2.1 History of NEC

Various parties from the insurance, electrical, and construction industries jointly introduced the NEC in 1897. The National Conference on Standard Electrical Rules was responsible for compiling the initial edition of electrical safety regulations. Representatives of numerous national groups attended the conference.

The primary topics covered in the NEC's first edition include the following:

- Single-disconnect device usage.
- Applications for insulated conduit
- How to identify the white wire

2.2 The National Electrical Code's Application

The NEC is designed to cover a broad range of electrical installations in domestic, professional, and industrial settings. The technical applications covered by the NEC are as follows:

- Installing electrical raceways, equipment, and wires.
- Installation of raceways and optical fiber cables.
- Raceways, tools, and conductors for signaling and communications.

2.3 Importance of NEC's Enforcement for Ensuring Workplace Safety

Electrical risks can result in serious physical harm and even fatalities. The equipment and the employees are at risk and in danger in workplace situations that DON'T meet

NEC regulations. You might be surprised to understand that many workers are unaware of these dangers. Hazardous electrical installations are occasionally reviewed and fixed only after a significant accident occurs. People within a facility and those around are in grave danger from arc bursts, shocks, and flashes.

What is the secret to making sure there is utmost safety? The keys to safety are consistent instruction, awareness, and enforced compliance. Financial factors and production indicators should not be used as an excuse for non-compliance. Failure to follow NEC regulations is illegal in many jurisdictions under federal law. Criminal charges or hefty fines may be brought against the responsible organizations. All levels of staff must be included in electrical safety programs, which are essential for assuring employee protection.

2.4 NEC Adoption in Electrical Installations

To safeguard the lives of citizens or employees from potential electrical threats and to prevent legal action, cities and states create and put into practice a single set of electrical standards. Therefore, to begin working as licensed professionals, electricians from around the nation participate in extensive training that complies with the NEC regulations. Through a procedure that turns the NEC into legislation, the majority of states and their various authorities accept and enforce the code. Violation of the NEC is prohibited. Modifications may be made depending on how the relevant jurisdiction interprets a particular rule. The majority of states and localities follow the recommendations made by the NFPA's panels, which are comprised of highly competent members of the technical committee.

2.5 Structure of NEC

The NEC code is made up of nine chapters, an index, and annexes. It covers various topics related to electrical safety and regulations, including enforcement, guidelines, scope, and objectives. The NEC Handbook also includes several cross-references, supplemental pictures, and explanations to aid experts in understanding the code. The National Electrical Code addresses branch circuit regulations, in particular, the use of fixtures and receptacles. The NEC establishes the minimum number of branch circuits that must be present in a site and the required distance between outlets in electrical applications. The criteria vary depending on the type of application, the purpose, and the region.

CHAPTER 3
ELECTRIC SAFETY MEASURES

When working with electricity, safety precautions are essential. Basic ground rules must be followed before compromising security. You can work safely with electricity by following the following fundamental safety rules.

3.1 Common Safety Measures

Did you realize that a typical home or company's voltage and available current of electricity is powerful enough to result in electrocution death? Any electrical system has the potential to be dangerous. Because it naturally conducts electricity, your body is susceptible to burns and shocks.

These consist of thermal burns, which impact both the skin's surface and interior organs, and explosions, which can constrict your muscles and your lungs, perhaps leading to a severe accident. Direct contact with electrically charged conductors or circuit components may disrupt the brain's functioning, make breathing difficult, or even cause your heart to stop.

Electricity work is a big undertaking!

These are the eight crucial safety precautions to be aware of and respect whether you are through electrician certification or are about to start an apprenticeship.

1. Stay Away from Power Lines

Construction sites frequently have power lines nearby, which is dangerous for electricians and other professionals. Although there are no visible or sparking wires on the connection, thousands of volts of electricity can be transmitted into your body with just a simple touch. Electrocution from a power line can result in heart failure, fourth-degree burns on your body, or the amputation of a limb.

Becoming acquainted with your area's power line regulations is crucial. For instance, the Ontario Health and Safety Act establishes minimal separations that must be kept based on the line's voltage. Before digging, you should check the placement of any power lines, and you are restricted to using your hands when you are less than 1m from a power line.

7. A Person Who Has Been Electrocuted Shouldn't Be Touched

It's perfectly normal to want to help someone you know who has been electrically burned or shocked. But keep in mind that the body acts as a conductor. If you interact with anyone shocked, the current will enter your body, putting both of you in danger. Turning off the main electrical supply should be your first step before dialing 911 for help in a critical situation. If you know about CPR, you can start treating the patient while you wait for the ambulance. Can't shut off the supply of power? Using a non-conducting substance like wood or plastic pushes the individual away from the interaction.

8. Select the Appropriate Ladder

Three elements are frequently used to make ladders: aluminum, fiberglass, and wood. Because they don't conduct electricity, the latter two choices are the best for electricians. Fiberglass is a good option because wood can deteriorate over time, especially if it is frequently exposed to damp surroundings. Despite being more costly, fiberglass staircases have a long lifespan that might save you.

9. Be Familiar With Electrical Codes

The National Electrical Code (NEC) is going to make up a significant portion of your training as an electrician in Canada. Its goals are to safeguard electricians and increase the safety of electrical equipment and installations. To ensure your safety while working, be aware of new regulations and best practices for wiring, repair, and construction.

10. Use the Appropriate Protective Gear

You must always wear safety clothing when working with electricity, regardless of whether you are an apprentice, pre-apprentice, or have years of experience. Goggles, line hoses, hoods, insulated gloves, blankets, sleeves, and non-conducting hard helmets are all common pieces of safety gear. Similar to your instruments, this equipment should be checked before usage and, if necessary, repaired or sent for disposal.

11. GFCIS Should Always Be Used in Damp Work Areas

When you labor near water, your risk of receiving an electric shock increase. Before starting any work in a damp or wet environment, don't forget to install GFCIs (Ground Fault Circuit Interrupters). When utilized in damp environments, ensure that all instruments and cables are grounded or connected to a GFCI-protected outlet. Before the circuit may reach the human body and do major damage, GFCIs will cut it off.

12. Comply With Appropriate Tagout/Lockout Methods

When starting an examination or maintenance project, you must first turn off the power at the switching box and secure the switch in the neutral position. The same holds for any machinery or equipment you could be maintaining.

Any electrician's program must include instructions on lockout and tagout procedures. It is crucial to make sure that equipment has been disconnected before repairs are done to reduce the risk of shock and electrocution. Are you unsure if a piece of machinery is turned on? Before you start your repair, use a tester to inspect the cables, the service panels outside the metallic covering, and any hanging wires.

13. Test and Maintain Your Electric Equipment

Before using a tool, you ought to check it out, and if it needs maintenance, you should cease using it immediately. Look for broken cables, visible wires, and broken or weak plugs on your electrical equipment. Watch out for the insulating material that covers your extension cables because it is particularly prone to harm. Watch out for harm to switches, trigger locks, and cracks in your tools' handles or body casings. Avoid the error of "just once more" using a damaged tool.

Put it out of use immediately, label it so nobody else utilizes it, and spend money on top-notch maintenance.

3.2 Electricians: Workplace Safety Guidance

Working with electricity is challenging. It's also not secure. Every day they leave for work, electricians run the risk of serious injury. Electricians set up the circuits, fittings, and electrical lines required to supply electricity. They are also responsible for keeping these parts in good condition after installation. Even if you think yourself a sophisticated expert DIYer because you've watched a few renovations shows, there is a high degree of risk whenever you operate with electricity.

Electricity poses risks such as burns, compressed lungs from arc explosions, and involuntary muscular contractions; so, they and the general public should exercise caution when handling electricity and electronic parts. There will be greater demand for electricians as more people will need power, and new alternative energy equipment needs to be built. Based on the BLS, employment of electricians is expected to increase by 9% through 2026. Safety becomes even more important because more people will endanger their physical well-being to provide us with electricity.

Experienced electricians take various basic steps to reduce the likelihood of dangerous accidents and lessen the harm that occurs when they do happen. Seven actions that electricians can do to preserve safety at work are listed below:

1. Observe Correct Techniques

Speaking of methods, maintaining safety while working is one of the reasons electricians choose particular methods. Electricians join training courses to master their trade properly. Inaccuracies still occur in all occupations, and as a beginning electrician, you may experience some physical discomfort, but it has a way of teaching you not to repeat mistakes.

2. Ensure You Have the Necessary Training before Beginning a New Job

This last piece of advice builds on the previous one. Have faith in your capacity to finish the job. Inform your supervisor if you don't feel ready or secure enough to take on a certain assignment so they can help you become familiar with it. You will undergo on-the-job training when you start working as an electrician because an electrician training program cannot adequately prepare you for everything you will meet in real-world experience.

Electricians can ensure safety at work in a variety of ways. Have these recommendations aroused your curiosity about becoming one of the greater than 628,000 technicians in the US? In that case, you only have to locate a training course that suits your requirements.

3. Become Familiar With Your Legal Rights

Your basic right is to have a safe workplace as an electrical worker or any other type of employee. Laws are in place to protect you, and the Occupational Health and Safety Administration (OSHA) was established to defend this constitutional right. The OSHA website is a wealth of knowledge that will assist you in brushing up on your worker rights or learning them if you don't already know them. Gaining knowledge will give you power and help keep you safe while working.

4. Test First, Then Touch

The only method to determine whether an electrical circuit or other component is secure to touch is to test it first. Using a multimeter is the simplest technique to check a component for the strength of the current. Every electrician's toolbox should have these necessary gadgets.

Using a multimeter, you may determine whether the current running through an electrical component is powerful enough to contact it. The reading is commonly given in volts. A multimeter reading might help you determine the likely problem when troubleshooting.

5. Use Machinery Only as Directed by the Manufacturer

Tools are available to carry out a specific task or combination of operations. Manufacturers make tools for certain purposes and skills. Misuse may result in damaged property or physical harm. A screwdriver is not a very good substitute for a multimeter.

6. Make Sure You Have the Right Equipment

This complements the preceding readiness phase. Wearing enough durable safety equipment is one of the most crucial aspects of job safety. Your hands can be protected from electrical currents by wearing insulated gloves. Wearing a hard hat can assist in preventing injuries from dangling electrical wires and falling debris, such as in a construction environment. Additionally, ocular protection is crucial.

Another essential component of an electrician's professional apparel is flame-retardant gear because sparks and fires caused by sparks frequently occur during routine operations. If you're wondering whether your protective equipment complies with industry standards or not, OSHA gives detailed rules for what constitutes adequate PPE when working with electricity. The use of personal protective equipment is the first step of defense if something goes wrong.

7. Prepare for Anything

The key to minimizing the possibility of a dangerous accident is planning. It's crucial to evaluate the type of project you're currently working on and what may go wrong during its execution. Is there even a remote possibility that such-and-such a circumstance will occur? If it does, you'd better carry something to handle it. You can prepare for the unexpected when it eventually occurs by taking the time to carefully consider such scenarios and make the necessary plans.

8. Get Involved in Your New Career

Coyne College, one of Chicago's premier institutions for skilled-trade education, offers electrical installation, management, and development and maintenance programs. To better meet the demanding schedules of its students, Coyne College provides both programs during the day and at night. The Coyne College campus, which is located in the Chicago Loop at the corner of State and Madison Streets, offers both programs.

In comparison to the electrical construction maintenance program, the curriculum for the electrical construction and planning program is more thorough and can be finished in as few as 78 weeks. However, depending on whether you attend day or night classes, the electrical construction and maintenance program can be completed in 42 to 56 weeks while still preparing you for the field. You will be immersed in courses like these as an electrical program student at Coyne College.

- Principles of Electricity and Electronics
- Safety of Electrical Tests and Equipment
- Residential Electrical Architecture
- Electrical Theory and Applications

The highly qualified instructors at Coyne with years of practical expertise will teach you the detail of the electrician trade in an atmosphere centered on your achievement.

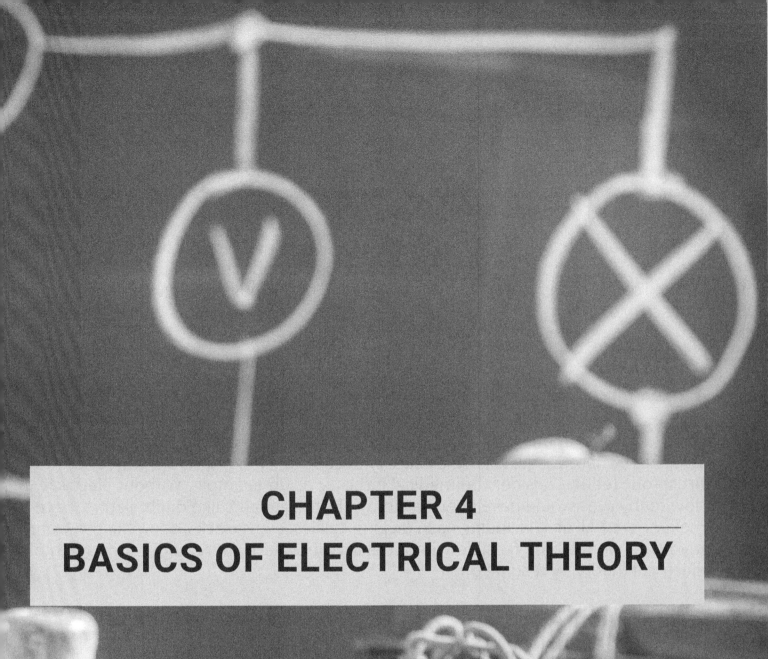

CHAPTER 4
BASICS OF ELECTRICAL THEORY

A successful electrician needs various skills, practice, and physical requirements. You must also hone your communication and reading skills to succeed as an electrician.

Every aspiring electrician needs to have a firm understanding of electrical theory. Electricity can be tasteless, soundless, and invisible. So, to keep yourself and others safe, you need to comprehend it theoretically.

Understanding how electrical equipment works will help you ensure it is installed properly. There is much to learn to properly understand the theoretical side of electricity. To become licensed electricians, the candidates must also advance their math and science skills.

4.1 Learning Fundamental Electrical Theory

Electricity has had the greatest impact on our culture, way of life, and ability to survive. Everywhere we go, we use electricity to cook our food, light our way, and even brush our teeth. Consider the medical industry as an example. Without electricity, how many lives would have been saved by electric gadgets like defibrillators, pacemakers, etc.? All of it, including hash tagging, talkies, eight-tracks, and yelling, "I want my MTV," wouldn't be feasible without electricity. Learn more about fundamental electrical theory by reading on.

1. Electricity: What Is It?

Consequently, what is electricity, and where does it originate from? What's more, why is it undesirable to combine carpet, socks, and a doorknob? Electricity can be identified as the movement of charge, which is typically thought to be from positive to negative. The motion of the discharge is electricity, regardless of whether the charge is produced chemically (as in batteries) or physically (via friction from socks and carpet).

2. Learning Electric Charge

Atom mobility is electricity. We can use the charge produced by electrons to do tasks. Your phone, stereo, lamp, and other devices use the motion of atoms to carry out work. The motion of electrons serves as the same fundamental power source for all of them. Electrons, or more precisely, the charge they generate, can be used to explain the three fundamental concepts:

- The passage of charge is measured as current.
- The variation in charge between two places is known as voltage.
- Resistance is a material's propensity to oppose current flow (charge flow).

As a result, when we discuss these numbers, we discuss the flow of charge and, consequently, the behavior of electrons. A closed circuit permits the transfer of charge from one location to another. Thanks to the circuit's components, we can manage and use electricity to generate power. A scientist from Bavaria named Georg Ohm specialized in electricity. He begins by defining a resistance unit that is determined by voltage and current. Let's begin with voltage and work our way up.

3. Voltage

The "pressure" that moves electrons is referred to as voltage whose SI measurement unit is volts denoted as V. Moreover, higher voltage means high power is being delivered to the electronic device.

However, an inadequate voltage may cause trouble because it may hinder the functioning of the circuit causing problems in attached devices. Hence, the person should have sufficient knowledge of electronics to properly troubleshoot the challenges that arise with the device.

4. Current

Electric current is the name given to this movement of electric charge. Alternating current (AC) and Direct current (DC) are the two different current forms. While AC is current that regularly changes its direction and voltage polarity, DC is current that runs in a single direction with a constant voltage polarity. DC pioneers Thomas Edison and Alessandro Volta contributed significantly to the development of electricity. However, the efficiency of using DC over large transmission distances decreased as societies evolved. With the development of alternating current electrical systems, Nikola Tesla transformed everything. It is possible to generate the high voltages required for lengthy transmissions using AC. As a result, most modern portable electronics run on DC power, whereas power plants generate AC.

5. Ohm's Law

Ohm's law, also known as V=IR, is the most fundamental law of electricity. Voltage, or the potential difference between two charges, is determined by the V. It is a measure of the effort necessary to move one charge between two places, to put it another way. The potential difference between two points of reference is measured when we see a number like 10 Volts. The two voltages can be any voltage difference between +5V and -5V, +20V, and +10V, etc., but typically they will be +10V and 0V (also known as ground).

The phrase "natural grounds" may be used in the field to describe a system in which all devices use an identical zero-point reference (or ground) to guarantee that the same potential difference (or voltage) is utilized across the system. The second element of Ohm's law is the electrical current, which has a measurement unit of amperes and is represented in the formula by the incredibly logical symbol I. As was already mentioned, current measures the passage of electrons in a circuit. The letter R, which stands for resistance, is all that is left. The unit of measurement for the amount of current resistance in a circuit is electrical resistance, expressed in Ohms. Resistance merely prevents the flow of current.

Heat is created by friction that happens when electrons move against the resistance in the circuit. The light bulb is the circuit component where resistance is used the most frequently. A circuit created by the light bulb experiences enough resistance that the filament inside heats up and emits light. A circuit's resistance might be used when changing voltage levels, current pathways, etc. It is usual practice to separate voltage levels using resistors, independent containers of resistance that can be added to a circuit.

6. What Is Electric Power?

Electric power refers to the rate at which electrical energy is transferred or consumed. It is the flow of electrical energy in an electrical circuit. Electric power is measured in units called watts (W) and represents the amount of work done or energy transferred per unit of time.

In simple terms, electric power is the product of voltage and current. The voltage, measured in volts (V), represents the electric potential difference or the force that pushes the electric charge through a circuit. The current, measured in amperes (A), represents the flow of electric charge. The formula of power is given below.

P = Electric Power

V= Potential difference

I= Electric Current

Now, I would like to discuss a couple of other circuit ideas. We must first comprehend what series and parallel circuits are.

7. Kirchhoff's Voltage Law

The law states that the total amount of voltages present in any complete electrical loop equals the sum of voltage drops inside that similar loop, which is also zero. In other terms, inside the loop, all of the voltage's algebraic sum is zero. Kirchhoff's theory is also known as the Conservation of Energy.

8. Kirchhoff's Current Law (KCL)

Kirchhoff's Current Law (KCL) stipulates that no charge is lost within a node since there is no other place for it to go and states that the overall current or charge entering a node or junction is precisely equal to the charge leaving the node. In other words, I(exiting) + I(entering) = 0; the algebraic sum of all leaving and entering currents from a node is equal to zero. The concept of Kirchhoff is frequently referred to as the conservation of charge.

Linear and nonlinear components are used to construct electrical devices. To comprehend these devices' underlying design, it is essential to have a rudimentary understanding of both linear and non-linear circuits.

4.2 What Is a Switch?

A switch is the most frequent device used daily to turn off and turn on electrical appliances, including fans, lighting, coolers, and air conditioners. A switch has the power to complete or disrupt a circuit. In a circuit, electricity can flow as long as the switch is ON.

There are many different switches available, but in this post, we will talk about the one-way switch and the two-way switch, as well as the main distinctions between them.

1. A One-Way Switch

A one-way switch is one that only permits current to flow in one direction, meaning that it does not conduct while the current is flowing in the opposite direction. It has two terminals to create or interrupt an electric circuit. The one-way switch is said to be in the "ON state" when the connection is made, and current is said to flow through it. The switch breaks the circuit when it is in the "OFF" position, and no electricity passes through it. One-way switches are used when a single location control is required for an electric device. They are frequently used to control fan operations, lighting, AC, coolers, etc., from a single location in homes, offices, enterprises, etc.

2. A Two-Way Switch

A switch type with three terminals is a two-way switch. A two-way switch is essentially two one-way switches combined into one single device. The two-way switch has two conductors that can go either way. One terminal of a two-way switch is connected to another when it conducts. Still, the third terminal has a broken connection, meaning that all three terminals of a two-way switch cannot be concurrently connected. The two-way switch is a unique and little-used form of switch. It is mostly used for controlling the lamps in wiring for stairways, lengthy corridors, etc. A two-way switch from two distinct places can control one electrical device.

4.3 Branch Circuits

The cabling that connects a home's equipment to the circuit breaker is known as a branch circuit. The final electrical wiring from your electricity provider to the home's appliances is found in these circuits. Although branch circuits come in many shapes and sizes, they are all a sort of wiring that supplies electricity to a home and serves as a safety feature to make sure all appliances run on a reliable, safe supply of power. The branch circuits in a home belong to the homeowner because they go beyond the circuit breaker. The electrical company owns all wiring that runs through the circuit breaker from underground, but any wiring that continues past the breaker belongs to the homeowner. Because of this, replacing or fixing defective branch circuits in residences may fall under the responsibility of the homeowner. When dealing with these circuits, it's essential to keep note of how many amps each circuit uses so you can replace them with the appropriate kind of wire.

1. Working on Branch Circuit

Branch circuits function by supplying outlets and devices in a home with power from the circuit box. They are connected to the circuit breaker and the power company's subterranean wires. These power cables provide electricity to a home, and once it is in the hands of a homeowner, it is transferred by branch circuits to each outlet. Branch circuits enable you to power any gadget in a household by connecting the electrical system to the power a service provider offers.

2. Branch Circuit Design

The design of the circuits that provide power to various rooms in a home is referred to as branch wiring design. The service distribution panel, which has two hot bus bars and a neutral bus bar, is where the branch wire is connected. Depending on the amount of electricity needed, a circuit may be connected to either the hot bus bar, the neutral bus bar, or even both. For instance, only the neutral bus bar and one hot bus bar need to be connected for a circuit delivering 120 volts of power. On the other hand, both hot bus bars must be connected to a circuit that delivers 240 volts of power.

3. Types of Branch Circuit

There are six different types of branch circuits.

When working with a home's electrical system, it may be crucial to ensure that you understand the type of wiring that goes with each circuit and what it powers. Following are six distinct branch circuit types and their functions:

I. CIRCUITS FOR LIGHTING

Branch circuits, known as lighting circuits, supply electricity to a home's lights. When you flip the light switch, these circuits supply power to the ceiling-mounted lights in every room. Depending on a home's size, there could be separate lighting circuits for each room or just one for the whole thing. One lighting circuit is frequently present on each level in multi-story homes, which makes it easier to identify problems with one if there are any.

II. CIRCUITS WITH 120 VOLTS

One of the two primary categories of branch circuits is a 120-volt circuit. All the typical outlets and lighting fixtures in a house receive power from 120-volt circuits connected to the electrical wiring in the building. Because they supply power to systems that don't require a lot of electricity, these circuits are the low-power equivalent of branch circuits. It can be crucial to avoid overloading a 120-volt circuit when making repairs because they might be unable to supply power to numerous large pieces of equipment simultaneously.

III. Circuits for Outlets

Outlet circuits power the electrical outlets in a home. Depending on the home's layout and size, several outlet circuits run throughout the building, or just one circuit powers every outlet simultaneously. If you experience any issues with either type, combining outlet circuits with lighting circuits might be useful to reduce the damage to your electrical system.

IV. Circuits Using 240 Volts

The most potent main branch circuit type is a 240-volt circuit. These power large appliances and a home's central heating and cooling systems. You can use them to power multiple large appliances simultaneously since they produce twice as much power as 120-volt circuits. Considering that the 240-volt circuits can still only power a certain number of devices, avoid connecting too many gadgets to one circuit. Smaller gadgets could be harmed by using 240-volt circuits because a rapid burst of electricity can overwhelm them. Therefore, make an effort to place them securely and in the correct locations.

V. Specific Circuits for Appliances

One particular piece of equipment is powered via a branch circuit known as a dedicated appliance circuit. Large appliances that may need a lot of electricity, including refrigerators and air conditioners, can be powered by these circuits. It's crucial to connect only one device to these circuits to keep them operational and avoid any problems with the appliance they power.

VI. Circuits in the Room

Room circuits are circuits with branches that supply electricity to a particular room in a house. You can utilize room circuits to separate the flow of power into different sections because each one of them may have many lighting fixtures and plugs. If there is a problem with the electricity in one room, you might be able to trace it to that area's circuit; therefore, using these circuits might be a helpful approach to finding issues. This helps isolate problems in one room rather than numerous, which can help minimize electrical damage to a home.

4.4 Electric Circuit

It is a closed-loop network that offers a channel for the current to return to its starting point. A circuit is a closed conductor through which current can flow. An electrical network or electrical circuit is another name for an electric circuit.

An electrical circuit is made up of several active and passive parts that make up an electrical network, such as resistors, capacitors, inductors, diodes, transistors, etc. Electric current flows in a closed-loop circuit from the source (such as a battery) via the conducting material (such as wires and cables) to the load (such as a light bulb) and then back to the source.

1. Electronic Circuits: What Are They?

To further distinguish an electronic circuit from an electrical circuit, at least one active component must be included in the circuit, which is a sort of electric circuit made up of numerous electronic components like diodes, transistors, resistors, capacitors, etc. In this manner, it ceases to be an electrical circuit and becomes an electronic circuit.

2. An Electrical Network

An electric network is a collection of various electrical elements and parts interconnected in any way (simple or complicated arrangement). Although the phrase is the same for an electrical circuit, it is most frequently used to refer to complicated networks that network theorems may solve.

3. What Are Complex Networks?

A complex network is a circuit that has many electrical components and elements that are intricately designed, including resistors, capacitors, inductors, current and voltage sources (both AC and DC), and resistors. Simple Kirchhoff's or Ohm's laws cannot be used to address these types of networks. In that case, the number of equations will be more obvious.

The simplest way to solve and analyze a complicated network is to use particular methods like network theorems, such as Thevenin's theorem, Norton's theorem, Superposition theorem, star-delta transformation, super node, and super mesh circuit analysis, etc.

4. Components of Electric Circuits

The essential components of a perfect electric circuit are:

- Electric generators and batteries are the main electrical sources used to supply electricity to the circuit.
- Load.
- Switches, circuit breakers, MCBs, and other devices resembling potentiometers are the major controlling devices used to regulate electricity.
- Conducting paths are used in circuits to move electric current from one point to another, often wires or other conductors.
- Electric fuses, MCBs, and switchgear systems are the most common protection devices that shield the circuit from abnormal circumstances.

5. Characteristics of Electric Circuits

Electric circuits' fundamental characteristics include the following:

- There is always a closed path, a circuit.
- There could be a potential dip across the various elements due to the current flow.
- There is always at least one energy source in a circuit serving as an electron source.
- From the positive toward the negative terminal, conventional current flows.
- Some electric components are controlled and uncontrolled energy sources, resistors, capacitors, inductors, etc.
- Electrons move from the negative terminal toward the positive terminal in an electric circuit.

6. Electric Circuit Types

The following are the types of electric circuits.

I. Parallel Circuit

This circuit has numerous channels for electricity because all electrical components (such as voltage and current sources, inductors, capacitors, resistors, etc.) are linked in parallel. The bare minimum number of branches in this circuit is two.

II. Series Circuit

These are single-branch circuits since all electrical components (such as voltage or current sources, inductors, capacitors, resistors, etc.) are in series.

III. Parallel-Series Circuit

Series-parallel circuits have elements connected in series in some places and parallel in others. In other words, this circuit combines series, parallel, and series-parallel circuits.

IV. Closed Circuit

A closed circuit contains a return path for current to pass through it (also known as a completed circuit).

V. Open Circuit

An open circuit isn't closed or one that doesn't have a way for current to return. In other words, a circuit is said to be open when the voltage tends to the EMF (of the generating source) and no current is flowing at all.

VI. Short Circuit

A circuit with a return channel where current can flow, and resistance is equal to zero. A short circuit is a term for a finished or closed circuit without a connected load. In other terms, a short circuit is a circuit where the voltage tends to 0, and the current tends to infinity.

VII. Star and Delta Circuit

Circuits of this type are linked using a connection known as a star or a delta connection. Electrical components are connected in these circuits in ways that are not well defined in terms of series, parallel, or series-parallel arrangement. Star to Delta transformation and Delta to Star transformations can be used to solve star delta circuits.

You must know about the following terminology that describes a circuit's nature and features before you may analyze an electric circuit or network.

VIII. DC Circuit

DC circuits are any electrical circuits that use a power supply source. Battery packs and DC generators are two examples of supply sources.

IX. AC Circuit

The term "AC circuit" refers to a circuit with an AC supply source of voltage. Synchronous generators and alternators are two examples of supply sources.

X. Circuits with a Single Phase

Single-phase AC supply is the type of AC electricity where all voltages have the same sinusoidal pattern at a certain time. Two wires—the phase or line and Neutral—must complete a single-phase AC circuit.

XI. Circuits in Polyphase

Poly indicates there are several. As the name implies, three sinusoidal voltages with a 120° phase difference make up the AC power. Three- or three-phase four wires are required to complete a three-phase AC circuit.

7. Circuit's Constants, Parameters, and Other Related Expressions

Circuit constants imply too many parts or elements utilized in electrical paths, such as capacitance, resistance, frequency, inductance, etc. These variables can be distributed or combined.

I. The Passive Circuit

Passive Circuit Unilateral and Bi-lateral Circuits are circuits without any EMF sources.

II. Active Circuit

An active circuit has one or more EMF (Electromotive Force) sources.

III. Linear and Non-Linear Network Circuits

Linear Network Circuits

In simple terms, we can state that a linear circuit is a circuit of electricity with constant properties such as resistance, inductance, and capacitance. Alternatively, we may argue that a linear circuit is one in which the parameters do not change about the voltage and current.

The word "linear" typically refers to a straight line that resembles a diagonal and describes linear properties between voltage and current. In other words, the voltage directly relates to the current flow in the circuit. Current flow in the circuit likewise increases with an increase in voltage, and vice versa. The figure below depicts the linear circuit's output characteristics between current and voltage.

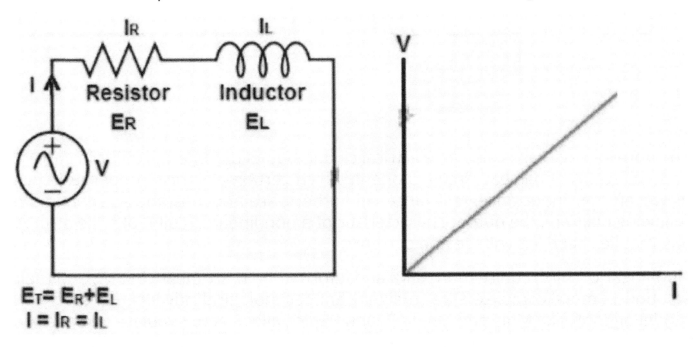

$E_T = E_R + E_L$
$I = I_R = I_L$

The response of the output in a linear circuit is inversely proportional to the input. The voltage between the two places in the circuit is sinusoidal with frequency "f," just like the applied sinusoidal in the circuit.

Non-Linear Network Circuits

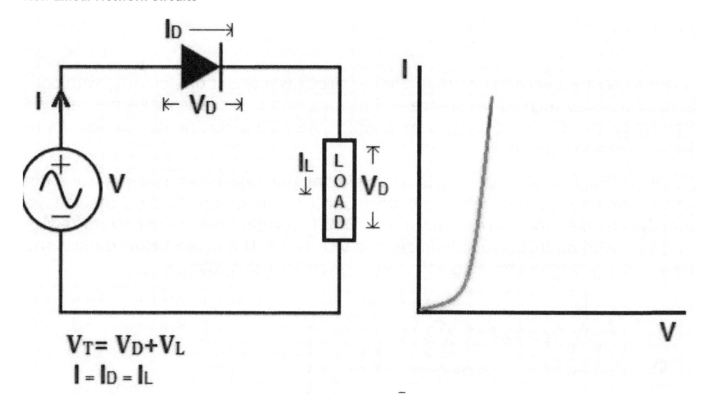

$V_T = V_D + V_L$
$I = I_D = I_L$

The non-linear circuit is also an electrical circuit, but its parameters differ in current and voltage. A non-linear circuit is one in which certain electrical properties, such as waveforms, inductance, resistance, and others, are not constant. As seen in the following diagram, the output characteristic of a non-linear circuit looks like a curve line that lies between voltage and current.

Non-linear circuits require more data and information than linear circuits, and their solution is more complex. Due to significant technological advancements, circuit modeling tools like Multisim, MATLAB, and PSpice allow us to simulate and analyze the output curves of both linear and non-linear circuits.

IV. UNIDIRECTIONAL AND BI-DIRECTIONAL CIRCUITS

Unidirectional Circuits

When the supply voltage or current changes direction in unilateral circuits, the characteristics of the circuit also change. In other terms, a unilateral circuit only permits one direction of current flow. Because they do not execute rectification in both supply directions, a diode or a rectifier is an example of a unilateral circuit.

Bi-directional Circuits

When the direction of the supply voltage or current changes in bilateral circuits, the characteristic of the circuit remains constant. A bilateral circuit enables electrons to flow in each direction. The most suitable illustration of a bilateral circuit is a transmission line since it can provide a source of voltage from either the starting end or the concluding end while maintaining consistent circuit characteristics.

8. Electric Circuits and Networks Related Terms

I. NODE

Node, or an equipotential section in a network, is the connection site of more than one active element (sources, voltage, current sources), passive elements connection such as an inductor, resistor, capacitor, etc., or circuit elements.

II. BRANCH

The branch is simply the name for the area of an electric circuit between two connections. One or more parts can be joined and have multiple terminals in a branch.

III. LOOP

A loop may contain several meshes and is a closed channel in an electric circuit where one or more than two meshes can be followed. The circuit must be in the closed route to constitute a loop. It must contain a minimum of one loop to be considered complete.

IV. MESH

A mesh is a closed path without any additional loops. It is a term used to describe a closed loop without any other loops inside of it or a path without any other paths.

4.5 What Is Feeder?

It is the power line in which electricity is transmitted in power systems, and feeders are utilized for this purpose. It transmits power from the generating station or substation to the distribution stations. Since there is no intermediate tapping, the sending and receiving sections will experience an identical current flow. We might obtain constant voltage from feeders, which are conducting devices that transmit power to the main load center.

1. Feeder Design for Power System

The majority of feeders are made up of raceways-enclosed cables. Raceways are confined channels created to accommodate wires, cables, or busbars. Conduit, a pipe that can be rigid or flexible and constructed of conducting or non-conducting material, is the most popular kind of raceway. Three factors are taken into consideration while choosing the feeder conductor's size:

- The load's continuous current rating.
- Voltage regulation.
- Greatest faults short-circuit current rating.

2. Types of Feeders

There are four different types of distribution feeder systems.

I. Radial Feeders

It can only be utilized when the generating station or substation is located in the middle of the consumers because this type of feeder emits electricity from the generating stations or substations, and it goes to the distributors at the other end. It is used for many distribution processes and is very affordable and simple. Thus, the power is only flowing in one way.

II. Parallel feeder

A drawback of radial feeders is that there will be no supply for many customers if a fault occurs during the gearbox. This can be changed by using parallel feeders, which cost more because they have more feeders. However, they can be used to transfer heavy loads.

III. Ring Main

We could get the same level of reliability in this form of feeder system as we would in a parallel one. The distribution transformers are connected to two feeders in this type of feeder, which is employed in urban and industrial settings. If there is a problem, the power is transmitted to the substations from the same area where cabling has been completed for several routes. There won't be many fluctuations in the customer sector because a circuit breaker isolates the ring, and the supply will continue using a ring feeder. If a problem does arise, there is always a backup plan.

IV. Interconnected System

More than one substation or generating station powers the ring feeder in this form, making it a linked distribution. If the transmission fails, the system keeps running and transmits the load.

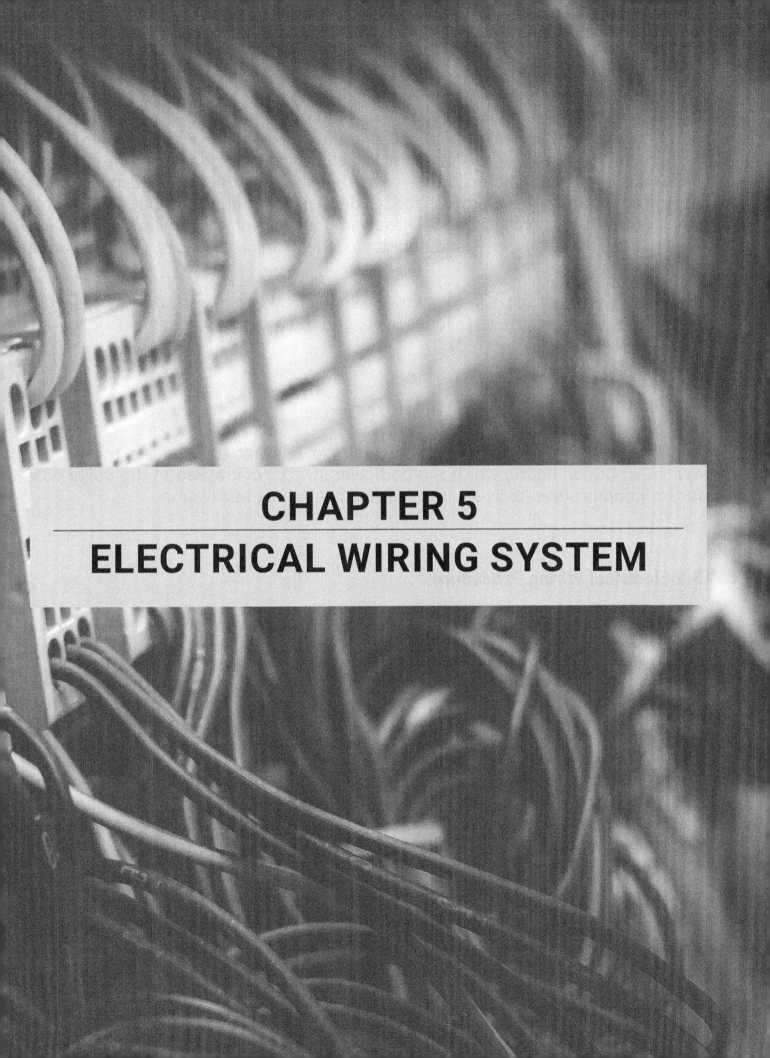

CHAPTER 5
ELECTRICAL WIRING SYSTEM

Many rules, regulations, and legislations have helped to standardize electrical wiring systems. Electrical rules and standards require that electrical wiring be installed properly and safely. If electrical wiring is done improperly or without according to any standards, it may result in short circuits, electric shocks, damage to the device or appliance, or gadget malfunction, which further shortens the item's lifespan. Before beginning the installation process for residential, commercial, or industrial wiring, some points must be considered. These variables include the construction type of the building, the ceiling, wall, and floor types, the wiring techniques, the installation specifications, etc.

Let's briefly go over some fundamentals of electrical wiring, including its idea, the procedures required, the techniques used, and the most prevalent types of wiring.

5.1 Electrical Wiring

The process of connecting wires and cables to relevant components toward the main distribution board, which is a particular structure attached to the utility pole for continuous power delivery, is called electrical wiring installation.

5.2 Electrical Wiring Procedures

Electrical wiring connects various accessories for distributing electrical energy from a provider's meter board to domestic appliances like lamps, fans, and other devices. This can be done using two methods, which we will discuss below:

1. Jointing System, Joint Box, or Tee

Connections to devices are created through joints when using this wiring technique. These joints are created in joint boxes by using appropriate connectors or joint cutouts. This wiring technique doesn't use a lot of cables. You might assume this wiring method is more affordable because it uses less cable. Of course, the savings from not purchasing cables will be utilized to purchase joint boxes, making the situation balanced. This approach is inexpensive and ideal for temporary installations.

2. A System With a Loop-in or Loop

Anywhere wiring is done, this procedure is employed. Lamps and other devices are connected in parallel to allow for individual control of each appliance. The feed conductor is looped in when a connection is needed at a light or switch by carrying it directly to the terminal and then back to the next location that needs to be fed. From one point to the next, until the last on the circuit is reached, the switch and light feeds are transported around the circuit in a series of loops. Neutrals are looped either in the switchboard or from a lamp or fan, while the phase or line conductors are looped either in the switchboard or box. Never loop a line or phase from a light or fan.

5.3 Electrical Wiring System Types

Whether a building is used for personal purposes (individual homes or apartments), huge business premises (office buildings), or industrial purposes (factories), electrical wiring is an essential component. Lighting and other power circuits use several electrical wiring techniques and systems. The kind of electrical wiring significantly influences the entire installation cost. Therefore, knowing what kind of electrical wiring systems are appropriate for a given work is crucial.

The following are some typical elements to take into account when selecting an electrical wiring system:

- Price of the wiring system
- Wire quality
- Kinds of wires and cables to be used
- Load type
- The wiring system's safety
- Future adjustments or extensions
- Installation duration
- Building materials (wood, concrete, brick, mortar, etc.)
- Safety from fire

The electrical wiring system should be able to guard against normal mechanical wear and tear under normal operating conditions, regardless of the type of wiring and the choice of wire. Typically, the electrical wiring systems (or at least their classification) are determined by the type of wire. The following are a few electrical wiring systems frequently used in residential, commercial, industrial, auditoriums, etc.

1. Cleat Wiring

In this, 0.6 m-diameter porcelain, wood, or plastic studs are fastened to walls or ceilings at regular intervals. Each cleat's hole is used to receive PVC insulated cables, which are then supported and held by the cleat.

Temporary installations use this form of wiring since it is less expensive. As a result, it is not appropriate for wiring in homes and is also an old technique.

2. Lead Sheathed Wiring

Except for the type of wire or cable, this wiring technique is comparable to the CTS / TRS Wiring. In this, vulcanized Indian rubber is used to insulate the electrical conductor before a sheath of lead-aluminum alloy (95% lead and 5% aluminum) is applied. This wiring is routed on wooden battens, much like the batten wiring, and is secured with tinned clips.

3. Casing and Capping Wiring

In this, a cable is passed through a grooved wooden casing. The wood enclosure is constructed with parallel slots that fit the cables and is prepared to be the desired fixed length. Screws are used to fasten the wooden casing to the walls or ceiling. A wooden cap with holes is placed on it to cover the cables once the cables have been inserted inside the casing's grooves. Although this wiring technique is equally inexpensive, there is an important possibility of fire in the event of short circuits.

4. Conduit Wiring

PVC cables are used in this wiring and are taken through either steel or PVC conduit pipes. Surface conduit wiring or concealed conduit wiring are both acceptable options for this process. Surface conduit wiring occurs when the conduit pipes run on the surface of the walls and ceilings. Concealed conduit wiring occurs when the conduits are covered with plaster and run inside the surface of the ceilings and walls. In industries, surface conduit wire is used to connect large motors. Contrarily, concealed wiring is the most prevalent and well-liked form of wiring residential structures. Conduit wiring is both the most secure and aesthetically pleasing technique of wiring.

5. Batten Wiring

Insulated wires are woven into the slender teak wooden battens of this. Plugs and screws secure the wooden battens to the walls or ceilings. Tinned brass link clips allow the wires to be attached to the battens. Nails and rust-resistant are used to attach these clips to the battens. In comparison to other electrical wiring systems, this kind of wiring connection is easy, inexpensive, and takes less time to complete. These are typically employed for installations inside. Tough Rubber Sheathed Wire (TRS) or Cabtyre Sheathed Wire (CTS) is typically utilized as the electrical conductor in this form of wiring.

5.4 Grounding of Electrical Systems

Ground, grounded, and grounding is frequently used when analyzing electrical infrastructure. These concepts have several official definitions that can be found in various standards and codes. But grounding connects the electrical system, electrical equipment, and metal enclosures to the earth, as its name implies. This connection to the earth is often referred to as "earthing."

1. A Review of Grounding Methods and Applications

Grounding is one of the most crucial yet least understood factors in the design of electrical systems. A relatively low impedance interconnection to the earth serves as grounding. Despite being a lousy conductor, the ground works well enough here. In addition to safeguarding humans, grounding is essential for the proper operation of electrical systems, whether they are used for electricity or electronics.

- System grounding assists in finding and fixing ground issues.
- Ground-fault current has a return path thanks to equipment grounding.
- Electrical conductivity and continuity are maintained by bonding.
- Wherever hazardous items are handled, static grounding lowers the risk of fires and explosions by preventing the buildup of static electricity.
- Grounding for lightning protection helps shield equipment and structures from direct hits.
- Surge arresters and overhead ground wires connected to the ground can reduce harmful system overvoltage to acceptable levels.

An electronic system can be grounded in the same way that any other electrical system can. However, caution must be used to avoid creating dangerous situations while using specific grounding procedures.

5.5 Electrical Boxes

Every home's electrical system depends heavily on electrical boxes. But because there are various kinds, it might be confusing for a homeowner. They are in various sizes and shapes, making it challenging to determine which box to employ for a certain purpose. The most typical types of electrical boxes are shown here to clear up any confusion.

1. Electrical Box Types

I. Junction Boxes

They are employed to join more than one electrical circuit or cable. They are available in several sizes to handle the required number of connections and cables. The size and rating of junction boxes must be appropriate for how much current they will be transmitting.

II. Waterproof Boxes

These outdoor-friendly boxes are used to house exposed electronics, including switches, outlets, and other gadgets. They frequently have a gasket or seal to keep moisture out and are composed of metal or plastic.

III. Outlet Boxes

Electrical outlets and receptacles are kept in these boxes. They come in various sizes to suit various types and numbers of outlets and can be mounted on a wall or ceiling. The size and rating of outlet boxes must also be appropriate for the amount of current they will be carrying.

IV. Floor Boxes

The purpose of these boxes is to supply electrical outlets on a building's level. They are frequently put in places like workplaces with elevated floors where running electrical lines through walls or ceilings is challenging. The current they will be carrying must be correctly rated for floor boxes, which come in several sizes and shapes.

V. Switch Boxes

Switches that regulate the current flow to various electrical equipment are kept in these boxes. Switch boxes are available in various sizes and, like outlet boxes, can be installed on a wall or ceiling. Additionally, they must be appropriately sized and rated for the current they will be transporting.

VI. Loading Centers

The main circuit breaker or fuse for an electrical system is in these boxes, called breaker boxes or panel boxes. They serve as a hub for transferring electricity across a structure and are often fixed on walls. To cope with the number of circuits and devices in a building, load centers are available in a range of sizes.

VII. Ceiling Boxes

These boxes store electrical equipment mounted on the ceiling, such as light fixtures, ceiling fans, and other devices. They are in various sizes and shapes and must be adequately certified for the weight of the electrical item being placed.

Along with these typical electrical boxes, there are specialized boxes for particular applications. For example, fire-rated boxes are used where a resistant-to-fire barrier is necessary, and safe from explosions boxes are used where explosive gases or vapors may be provided. No matter what kind of electrical box is used, it's critical to make sure it's sized and rated correctly for the amount of electricity it will be transporting.

5.6 Electrical Raceways

Any electrical system must consider the electrical raceways. It is a method for containing and shielding electrical cables and wires against harm from the outside. Additionally, raceways help organize cables and wires, making finding and handling them simpler. There are various possibilities when it comes to selecting a racecourse.

1. Types of Electrical Raceways

Different types of Electrical Raceways are given below:

I. Conduit Raceway

Conduit is one of the most popular kinds of electrical raceways. Metal or plastic tubes called conduit raceways store and safeguard electrical lines. Conduit raceways can be made of stiff metal, medium metal, stretchy metal, or non-metallic materials. The most robust alternative is a rigid metal conduit, frequently used in industrial environments. Medium metal conduits are appropriate for outdoor application since they are lighter in weight. Because they can bend and flex, flexible metal conduits are ideal for confined locations. Plastic or other non-metallic conduits are perfect for usage indoors and are constructed of PVC or other materials.

II. Cable Tray Raceway

Another well-liked alternative for arranging and safeguarding electrical lines is cable tray raceways. Metal or plastic trays, known as "cable trays," are intended to retain, support, and protect wires and cables. Cable tray raceways come in various designs, including ladder, wire mesh, perforated, and solid bottom. The rungs of ladder cable trays are meant to keep the cables in place. Small holes on perforated cable trays allow air to circulate. Smaller cables work best in wire mesh cable trays formed of wire mesh. The solid bottom of cable trays further protects cables.

III. Busways Raceways

Alternatives to conventional conduit and cable tray systems include busway raceways. Busbars, which are conductive bars that transport electrical current, are housed in metal enclosures called busway raceways. Busway raceways come in several configurations, including plug-in, feeder, lighting, and low voltage. Plug-in busway raceways are perfect for intermittent or changeable installations because they are made to be quickly connected and disconnected. Raceways for feeder and lighting busways are made to support heavier electrical loads. Raceways for low-voltage busways are made for low-voltage purposes, including data centers.

IV. Wireway Raceways

Conduits and wire ways raceways are similar. However, wire ways raceways have an insulated channel. Metal and plastic are just two materials that can be used to create wire ways. Wireways raceways come in various configurations, including ladder, ventilated, and non-ventilated. Cables are held in place by rungs that make up ladder wire ways. Small air-circulation holes can be found in ventilated wire ways. Cables are further protected and contained in non-ventilated wire ways.

2. The Best Raceway to Use for Your Electrical Requirements

The kind of wires or cables being used, the setting in which they will be set up, and the amount of electrical load being transmitted all play a role in selecting the best raceway. Consider the installation place, the surroundings, and the kind of cables or wires that will be placed when choosing a raceway. It's crucial to take future electrical system expansion or modifications into account.

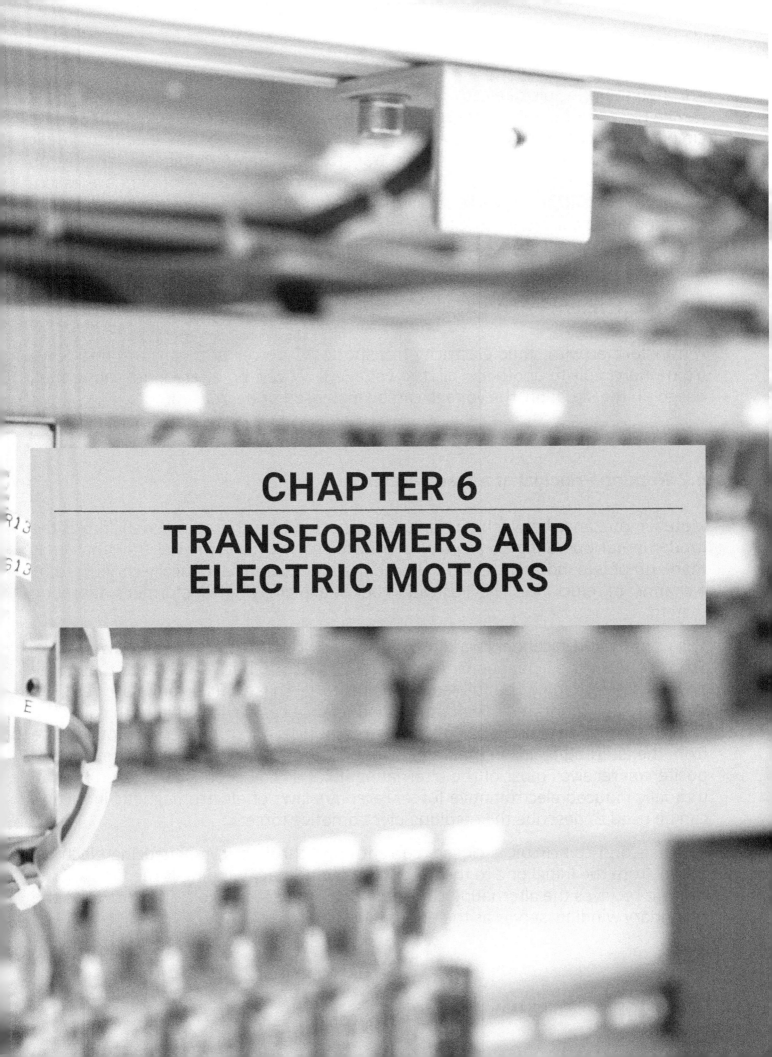

CHAPTER 6
TRANSFORMERS AND ELECTRIC MOTORS

Through the principle of electromagnetic induction, the transformer is the simplest device to convert electrical energy from one AC circuit to another circuit or several circuits. To increase or decrease voltage, a transformer uses the electromagnetic induction principle. Depending on the transformer, the AC voltage either goes up (step-up transformer) or down (step-down transformer). Transformers are essentially voltage control devices because they are typically used to transmit and distribute alternating current electricity.

6.1 Transformer

A transformer with static electricity transports AC power at a constant frequency from one circuit to another. Still, the voltage level can be altered, indicating that, based on the situation, the voltage can be increased or decreased.

6.2 Working Principal of a Transformer

Mutual inductance between two circuits connected by a shared magnetic flux is the fundamental operating concept of a transformer. A fundamental transformer is made up of two inductive, electrically independent coils magnetically connected by a channel of reluctance. The illustration below explains the transformer's operating system.

The primary and secondary windings of the electrical transformer are shown above. Strips connect the laminations that make up the core, but you can see that some tiny gaps are running the full length of the core. These offset joints are referred described as "imbricated." High mutual inductance can be found in both coils. The coil attached to an alternating voltage source induces a mutual electro-motive force from the alternating flux in the transformer installed in the laminated core. The opposite coil receives most of the alternating flux this coil produces, resulting in the mutually induced electromotive force. Faraday's laws of electromagnetic induction can be used to describe the resulting electromotive force:

If the second coil circuit is closed, current flows through it, magnetizing electrical power from the initial one to the other coil. The primary winding is the first coil because it receives the alternating current supply. The second coil, also known as the secondary winding, serves as the energy source.

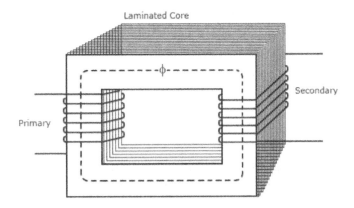

In essence, a transformer performs the following tasks:

» Electricity moves from one circuit to another.
» Electricity is transferred without changing frequency.
» The transfer is made using the electromagnetic induction method.
» Mutual induction connects the two electrical circuits.

5.3 Types of Transformers

1. Types of Transformers Based on the Core Material

In the electricity and electronics industries, various types of transformers are employed depending on the primary materials, which are:

I. Iron Core Transformer

The base of an iron core transformer is composed of several soft iron plates. The iron core transformer's powerful magnetic characteristics have an exceptionally high flux linkage. It has excellent efficiency as a result. The flexible iron core sheets are available in a range of dimensions and forms. E, I, U, and L are a few examples of common shapes.

II. An Air Core Transformer

An air core transformer's core is made of a substance that is not actually electromagnetic. Only the air-core transformer flux connection uses the air. An electromagnetic field is everywhere around an air-core transformer's principal coil as it produces an alternating current.

III. Toroidal Core Transformer

Examples of materials used in such types of transformers comprise iron or ferrite. Toroids, which feature a ring shape structure or donut-shaped base material, are commonly employed due to their high electrical properties. The ring shape produces little leaking inductance and exceptionally high inductance and Q factors.

IV. Ferrite Core Transformer

One is utilized in a ferrite core transformer because of its high magnetic permeability. This type of transformer has exceptionally low losses in high-voltage applications. Therefore, this kind of transformer is used in instances requiring high-frequency like RF-related applications, etc.

2. Types of Transformers According to Their Uses

Transformers are available in a broad variety of forms, each of which performs a specific function. Transformers can therefore be classified into the following groups according to their intended use:

I. Power Transformer

A larger power transformer is used to transport the energy to the substation or the main electrical supply. This transformer acts as a link between the main distribution grid and the power generator. Their power rating and specifications show that power transformers can be split into small, medium, and large groups.

II. Audio Output Transformer

The audio transformer is another common transformer in the electronics sector. It is primarily utilized in audio applications where impedance matching is required.

III. Measurement Transformer

A measurement transformer is sometimes referred to as an instrument transformer. Another measurement tool frequently used in the field of power domain is this one. A measuring transformer converts the voltage and current in a small ratio to its secondary output and separates the primary power.

IV. Pulse Transformer

Pulse transformers are among the most widely used PCB-mounted transformers for producing electrical pulses with constant amplitude. It is used in many digital circuits when isolated pulse generation is required.

V. Distribution Transformer

The distribution transformer performs the role of a step-down transformer, reducing high grid power to the required voltage for the end user, often 110V or 230V. The size of the distribution transformer may vary depending on the ratings or conversion capability.

3. Types of a Transformer According to Winding Configuration

I. Transformer With Auto-Winding

Although the main and secondary windings have traditionally been fixed, an auto-winding transformer allows for their series connection and the movement of the center-tapped node. By moving the center tap, the secondary voltage can be adjusted. The term "auto" is not an acronym for "automatic"; rather, it is used to alert the self or a single coil. By combining its primary and secondary parts, this coil generates a ratio. The position of the center tap node, which alters the output voltage, affects the main and secondary ratio. The most popular device is the VARIAC, which produces variable AC from a steady AC input.

4. Types of Transformers According to the Voltage Level

Based on the operating voltage, there are essentially two types of transformers. Some of them are as follows:

I. Step-Up Transformer

A step-up transformer raises the relatively low primary voltage to the secondary voltage. In this type of transformer, the proportion of the primary to secondary winding will be bigger than one since the primary winding has fewer turns than the secondary winding. Electronics stabilizers, inverters, and additional equipment that transform low voltage to a much greater voltage typically employ step-up transformers. In the process of distributing electricity, a transformer known as a step-up is also employed. High voltage is required for applications linked to power distribution.

II. Step-Down Transformer

Utilizing a step-down transformer, the primary voltage is reduced to a lower voltage across the secondary output. A step-down transformer has more windings on its primary side than its secondary side. The total secondary to primary winding ratio is always going to be less than one as a result. To provide minimal loss and cost-effective solutions, step-down transformers are employed in electrical systems that distribute electricity over great distances and run at extremely high voltages. High-voltage supply lines are converted into low-voltage supply lines using a step-down transformer. A step-up transformer is used in the grid to increase the voltage level before distribution.

6.4 Electric Motors

Electric motors are defined as electromechanical devices that transform electrical energy into mechanical energy. In simple terms, a motor is a device that generates rotational force. The interaction of the magnetic and electric fields is a key component in how an electric motor operates. The two main categories for electric motors are. The two types of motors are AC and DC. While a DC motor uses direct current as input, an AC motor uses alternating current.

6.5 Types of Electric Motors

Types of Electrical Motors are given below.

1. DC Motor

A device that converts electrical DC power into mechanical power is known as a DC motor. Its operation is based on the fundamental idea that when a current-carrying conductor is positioned in a magnetic field, a force is applied, and a torque is created. The self-excited and independently excited motors are the categories under which DC motors fall.

I. Self-Excited Motor

The Self-excited DC motor is further divided into three categories based on the connection of the field winding. They are the compound wound, shunt-, and series-wound DC motors.

Shunt Motor: A shunt motor is a type of motor in which the field winding is positioned parallel to the armature.

Short Shunt Motor: It is referred to as the motor's short shunt connection if the shunt field winding is parallel to the armature and not the series field.

Series Motor: The armature and field winding are linked in series in this motor.

Compound Wound Motor: A DC motor with a field winding connected in parallel and series is called a compound wound rotor. Short-shunt and long-shunt motors are additional categories for compound wound motors.

II. Separately Excited Motor

The term "separately excited DC motor" refers to a motor in which a separate DC source energizes the DC winding. The motor's armature winding is electrified and produces flux with the aid of a different source.

2. AC Motor

Alternating current is transformed into electrical energy by the AC motor. It can be broken down into three categories: induction motors, linear motors, and synchronous motors. Below is a detailed explanation of the motor.

I. Synchronous Motor

A synchronous motor refers to a device that converts alternating electricity into mechanical power at the desired frequency. The synchronous motor's speed is coordinated with the frequency of the supplied current. The poles and frequency of the motor determine the synchronous speed, which is measured in terms of the magnetic field's rotation. Reluctance and hysteresis motors are the two categories under which synchronous motors are categorized.

Hysteresis Motor: The hysteresis motor is a particular kind of synchronous motor that lacks a DC excitation system and has a consistent air gap. Hysteresis and eddy current in the motor work together to generate traction.

Reluctance Motor: This type of motor starts similarly to an induction motor and operates similarly to a synchronous motor.

II. Linear Motor

A linear motor generates linear force as opposed to rotational force. The rotor and stator of this motor are unrolled. Actuators and sliding doors both employ this kind of motor.

III. Induction Motor

The term induction motor refers to a system that under no circumstances operates at synchronic speed. This motor can produce mechanical power using electrical power via electromagnetic induction phenomena. There are two different types of induction motors based on the rotor's architecture. Specifically, phase wound and squirrel cage induction motors.

Rotor Squirrel Cage: A squirrel cage induction motor has a rotor of the squirrel cage design. The squirrel cage rotor lessens the rotor's magnetic locking and buzzing noise.

Phase Wound Rotor: This rotor is also referred to as a slip ring rotor, and the motor that employs it is referred to as a phase wound rotor.

The induction motor is divided into two sorts based on its phases. They are the three-phase and single-phase induction motors, respectively.

Induction motor with three phases: A three-phase induction motor is a type of motor that transforms three-phase AC electric power into mechanical power.

Induction motor with a single phase: A single-phase induction motor is a device that converts single-phase alternating current (AC) electric power into mechanical power using electromagnetic induction phenomena.

In addition to the motors mentioned above, numerous other specific machine kinds have extra features, such as stepper motors, DC, and AC servo motors, etc.

6.6 Starting Method of Induction Motor

An induction motor with three phases may start by itself. A revolving magnetic field is created when the supply is linked to the stator of a three-phase induction motor, which causes the rotor to start rotating and the induction motor to turn on. The motor slip is equal to one, and the current at the beginning is very significant. Not only does a starter start the motor, but it also serves the other two purposes. These are what they are:

- The strong beginning current will be decreased,
- They offer under and overload protection.

Start the three-phase induction motor by connecting it directly to the supply's full voltage. A lower voltage can also be applied to the motor to start it. The square of the applied voltage determines the induction motor's torque. As a result, a motor produces more torque when it is started at full voltage instead of a lesser voltage. The Cage Induction Motor can be started using one of three primary techniques. These are given below:

I. Direct On-Line Starter

An induction motor can be started directly online in a straightforward and affordable manner. The starter is connected directly to the source voltage using this technique. Small motors of 5 kW rating begin to operate via this technique to prevent supply voltage fluctuations.

II. Autotransformer Starter

In both a delta-connected and star-connected connection, the autotransformer is used. The autotransformer controls the induction motor's starting current.

III. Star Delta Starter

This method is the most popular and extensively used for functionalizing induction motors operating via three-phase. The motor operates using delta-connected stator windings in this technique.

The cage rotor induction motor uses the three starters mentioned above.

6.7 Slip Ring Starter Method

The complete voltage is supplied throughout the starter in a slip-ring induction motor starter. The supply current to the station is decreased as a result of the connection of the full starting resistance. As the motor's speed rises, the rotor resistance progressively disappears as the rotor starts to rotate. The starting resistances are eliminated, and the slip rings are short-circuited when the motor operates at its rated full load speed.

6.8 Maintenance of the Electric Motor

Despite having a similar appearance to other electrical components, electric motors significantly impact the viability and efficiency of the organization. To guarantee that electric motors always operate at their best, it is crucial to execute routine preventative maintenance inspections. Make an action plan focusing on checking and keeping an eye on the electrical wiring and motor as a starting point. This enables you to discover and recognize any issues the motor may experience and enables you to address these problems in advance. This will significantly reduce unforeseen repair costs. Given below are some tips for the maintenance of the electric motor.

1. Conduct Visual Checks

A short visual inspection of the electric motor can disclose some significant information. Examine its physical state and make a note of your findings. You can tell if the electric motor operates in a harsh environment by the corrosion and dirt buildup on particular parts. Look at the motor's windings for any indication of overheating, such as a burnt smell. Make sure that the contacts and relays are clean and free of rust. All of these elements could result in an internal issue because the debris could jeopardize the equipment's ability to function effectively.

14. Record Everything

Having documentation is crucial. Maintain thorough records of all preventative maintenance plans, tests, and outcomes. Keep track of every replacement and repair you make. Doing this gives you a more thorough knowledge of the machinery, helps recognize any problems, and helps you decide which components need to be replaced or fixed. Additionally, your documentation will be useful for upcoming inspections and audits.

15. Conduct a Commutator and Brush Inspection

Electric motors are less likely to experience irregularities or suddenly cease operation when subjected to routine maintenance examinations. Keep an eye out for usage and damage; even a small amount of excessive wear might cause the motor to have commutation issues.

16. Use Irradiation Therapy for Preventive Maintenance

Due to its favorable results, this inspection technique has recently gained popularity with predictive maintenance. Infrared thermography uses an infrared camera to take thermal pictures without affecting how the engine works. These photos show heat patterns at many locations across the electric motor at the same time, presenting a temperature profile of the motor. All mechanical systems have typical thermal patterns and a maximum temperature at which the motor may operate since they all create a specific quantity of thermal energy. The infrared camera will instantly detect issues such as inadequate airflow, insulation failure, or stator degradation. It will provide a thermal image of the unstable voltage to assist you in identifying its root cause and fixing it.

17. Perform Motor Winding Testing

You must test the motor's windings after you have examined all of the machine's parts. You can find any winding failures or irregularities using this test. Conduct a winding test of the motor if any suspicious noise or smell is noticed. The motor is disassembled as part of the examination to identify any irregularities. The items to check during this test includes insulation of the motor winding and rewinding.

18. Conduct Tests on Vibration

It cannot be easy to manually detect excessive vibrations. Moreover, the vibrations may be destructive to electric motors if not addressed promptly because it will decrease the lifespan of the motor by causing failure in its bearing and winding. The most common reasons for these vibrations may be excessive belts, tension ball bearings, unbalanced machinery, or damaged sleeves. You can test an electric motor by turning the belts off or on without any load.

19. Inspect the Bears

To detect potential issues, such as dirt accumulation, inadequate lubrication, and wear/tear, pay attention to noise and vibration originating in the bearings. If the housing of the bearing is too hot to touch, the motor may be overheating, or there may not be enough grease in the bearing. According to the location of the equipment, there are separate maintenance schemes for various bearing issues. It is important to note that we should know about the several types of bearings utilized in the manufacturing facility and the specifications for their repair.

6.9 Electric Motor Protection Devices

Electric motor supply circuits should typically be protected against overloading and breakdown currents. Any unsupervised motor should also be safeguarded against overloads, under-voltage, over-temperature, and fault currents.

All electric motors must also have an isolator and a control mechanism for stopping and starting. Installing fuses or circuit breakers in the switchboard, an electric motor starter with controls in a convenient place, and an isolator next to the electric motor typically satisfy all the requirements mentioned above. Modern proprietary motor starters can be found that include some or all of the requirements in a single device.

CHAPTER 7
CONTROL AND LIGHTING SYSTEM

7.1 Control System

A control system is described as a group of devices that coordinate, command, guide, or control other devices or systems' actions to produce a specific outcome. Control looping structures, a procedure created to keep a process variable at a particular set point, are how a control system accomplishes this. In other words, a control system can simply be defined as one that regulates other systems. The need for automation has grown along with the daily modernization of human civilization. Control over networks of interconnected devices is necessary for automation. In recent years, control systems have been increasingly important in the growth and development of contemporary technology and society.

Every part of our daily lives is influenced in some way, shape, or form by a control system. An air conditioner, a bathroom toilet tank, a refrigerator, an automated iron, and numerous automotive operations, including navigation, are examples of control systems in daily life. Control systems are used in industrial settings to regulate the quality of products, weapons systems, power systems, transportation systems, space technologies, robotics, and many other things. Both engineering and non-engineering fields can benefit from understanding control theory's fundamental ideas.

1. Characteristics of a Control System

The basic characteristic of a system for control is that the system's input and output should have a distinct mathematical relationship. A system is referred to as a linear control system when a linear proportionality can express the relationship between its input and output. Once more, a system is referred to as a non-linear control system when a single linear proportionality cannot express the relationship between input and output but rather when the input and output are associated by some non-linear relation.

2. Criteria for an Effective Control System

I. ACCURACY

Accuracy refers to an instrument's measurement tolerance and establishes the upper and lower bounds of errors that can be made under typical working circumstances. Using feedback elements helps increase accuracy. Any control system that wants to be more accurate should have an error detector.

xv. Oscillation

A few oscillations or continuous oscillations of the output often point to a stable system.

xvi. Sensitivity

A control system's parameters are constantly changing as a result of any changes to the environment, an internal disturbance, or other parameters. Sensitivity might be used to describe this change. Any control system should be sensitive to input signals and insensitive to such factors.

xvii. Speed

Speed is defined as the time the control system takes to provide a uniform output. A reliable system of control moves quickly. For such a system, the transitory duration is quite brief.

xviii. Noise

Noise is an unwanted input signal. For greater performance, a good control system should be able to minimize the noise effect.

xix. Bandwidth

The operating frequency range determines the control system's bandwidth. A good control system's frequency response should have the widest feasible bandwidth.

xx. Stability

One crucial aspect of the control system is stability. Such a control system is said to be a stable system. If the input signal is bounded, the output signal must also be bounded, and if the input signal is zero, then the output signal must also be zero.

3. Control System Types

Although there are many different kinds of control systems, they are all designed to govern output. Examples of control systems include those used to regulate things like position, temperature, velocity, pressure, acceleration, voltage, and current. The types of control systems are discussed below.

I. Open-loop Control System

The term "open-loop control system" refers to a control system where the control action is entirely independent of the system output. An open-loop control system also includes manual controls.

II. Closed-loop Control System

A closed-loop control system is one in which the output affects the input quantity in such a way that the input quantity adjusts itself in response to the output produced.

By offering feedback, an open-loop control system can be changed into a closed-loop control system. Due to outside disturbance, this feedback automatically modifies the output appropriately. A closed-loop control system is referred to as an automatic control system in this manner.

III. A Closed Loop Control System's Feedback Loop

A popular and effective tool when creating a control system is feedback. The feedback loop is the mechanism that allows the system to adapt its performance to achieve the desired outcome. It considers the system output. As a result, one signal is pulled from the output and fed back into the input.

The error signal is produced after this signal is compared to a reference input. The controller receives this error signal, and the output is then corrected. A feedback system is what one of these is known as. When the feedback signal is positive, A system is referred to as a positive feedback system. The error signal in a positive feedback system is created by adding the reference input signal and the feedback signal.

A system is referred to be a negative feedback system when the feedback signal is negative. The distinction between the reference input signal and the feedback signal in a negative feedback system provides the error signal. Any disturbance or alteration in the environment will have an impact on the output of any control system.

A type of radiant energy called light travels in waves of vibrating magnetic and electric fields. These waves have an oscillation frequency and a length, and the difference between these two quantities separates light from other types of energy on electromagnetic wavelengths. As observed on the electromagnetic spectrum, visible light is a condensed region between infrared energy (heat) and ultraviolet (UV). Sight is the term used to describe the visual experience that emerges from these light waves stimulating the eye's retina. So, you need both an eye that works and visible light to see.

7.2 Lighting System

Both nature and humans are capable of producing light. Lighting systems that convert electrical energy into light often create "artificial" light. Almost all lighting systems work by either running an electrical current through an element that glows after heating up or through gases that excite after running through it and release light energy. The first technique, incandescence, includes examples such as incandescent light sources. A filament receives current and heats up till it glows. Other light sources that rely on the gaseous discharge method have been developed, such as fluorescent, high-intensity discharge (HID), and low-pressure sodium light sources, as a result of the gaseous discharge method's perceived wastefulness (the majority of the energy entering the lamp leaves it as heat instead of visible light).

These light sources, often known as lamps, are typically found in lighting systems. A ballast is used to initiate and control the functioning of fluorescent, HID, and low-pressure neon lamps. The luminaire, or light fixture that contains the system and has other parts that spread the light in a predetermined pattern, is made up of lamps and ballasts.

7.3 The Lighting System's Design

A new lighting system must be created in a building or remodeling situation. The designer must first define the intended light levels for the activities that will be carried out in a specific area and then determine the light output that will be necessary to consistently achieve those goals, taking into account all the elements that cause both light output and light levels to deteriorate over time. Equipment must be selected and organized in a layout to provide the appropriate light distribution. Design decisions and equipment selected by the designer must also consider various quality elements, such as color, reducing glare, safety, and, if necessary, aesthetics.

7.4 The Lighting System Management

Many other types of people, from electrical contractors to facilities managers—in this case, we'll call them lighting managers—may be involved in the effective management of an existing system. The present lighting system must constantly offer the best lighting at the lowest operating and maintenance costs, according to the lighting manager's responsibility. A planned maintenance schedule to maintain the system performing at its best, retrofitting or updating the system to reduce energy costs and boost performance, and other measures that will guarantee that the lighting system is consistently doing its job are all examples of what this might entail.

7.5 Types of Lighting

1. Incandescent Lighting

Since they are common bulbs, many people are quite familiar with incandescent bulbs. There are many different sizes and voltages of these incandescent bulbs. When electricity flows through the tungsten filament within an incandescent light bulb, the filament glows and generates heat. This light bulb's filament can be immersed in a nitrogen gas mixture. Light-emitting fluorescent lights and other service-based novel innovations gradually replace these light bulbs.

This happens because when this light is turned on, a quick influx of energy and heat permeates the thin sections and heats the filament, which then tends to break and burn out the bulb. Incandescent light bulbs can be used with a controller and have a lifespan of 700–1000 hours. For household uses, incandescent lamps produce consistent heat, which is fairly good. About 15 lumens are produced per watt by an incandescent bulb.

2. Lamps With Low-Pressure Sodium

The low-pressure sodium lamp is the first sodium lamp that outperforms all other lighting systems in terms of efficiency. Similar to fluorescent bulbs, these lamps have a brief warm-up phase before reaching full brightness. Low-pressure sodium lighting is frequently employed in locations like roadways, walkways, outdoor spaces, and parking lots where color is not particularly significant.

3. Compact Lamps

Modern light bulbs that function similarly to fluorescent lamps are called compact fluorescent lamps. It has trouble being disposed of since it contains mercury. Incandescent light is intended to be replaced by a CFL. CFLs are generally energy-efficient, generate the same amount of light, and last a long time. Two or three tubular loops make up the majority of compact fluorescent bulbs. They even occasionally resemble incandescent lights quite a bit. These bulbs typically have a 10,000-hour lifespan and cannot be dimmed. A small fluorescent light has an efficiency of illumination of roughly 60 lumens per watt.

4. Lamps With High-Intensity Discharge

High-intensity discharge lamps include metal halide, mercury vapor, mercury self-ballasted lamps, and high-pressure sodium lamps. The interior glass tubes of these lamps, which contain tungsten electrodes and an electrical arc, are uniquely created. Metals and gas are both contained within this inner glass tube. Due to the self-ballasted lights' protection, extra equipment (starters and ballasts) must be provided to ensure that each bulb operates properly. Compared to fluorescent and incandescent bulbs, these lamps emit a lot of light. Medium-intensity burst lights are typically employed when high amounts of lighting are needed across significant areas, such as outdoor exercise areas, gyms, big public spaces, paths, streets, and garages.

5. Halogen Lighting

A halogen lamp is made up of a compact, transparent envelope sealed around a tungsten filament and contains an inert gas as well as a small amount of halogen (bromine or iodine). These lamps are more compact than regular lamps. The lifespan and brightness of the bulbs are both increased by halogen. A halogen light has a luminance efficiency of roughly 25 lumens per watt.

6. Neon Lights

A gas-discharge lamp with low gas pressure is a neon lamp. It is put together by arranging two electrodes inside a tiny glass encasement. High-brightness lamps are filled with pure neon gas, while standard brightness bulbs are filled with a mixture of argon and neon gas. The gas ionizes and begins to glow when a voltage is applied, enabling very little current to flow from one single electrode to another. Once the gas ionizes, a lower voltage can keep the lamp running. The sustaining voltage may range from 10 to 20 volts depending on the lamp and operational current.

7. Metal-Halide Lighting

An arc tube or discharge tube is housed inside a metal halide lamp's bulb. Mercury, MH salts, and a starting gas are all contained in this quartz or ceramic tube. One of the most effective lamps is the metal halide lamp, which produces a lot of light for its size. These lamps' most typical commercial applications include outdoor lighting systems, traffic lights, stages, and halls.

8. Fluorescent Tube

A fluorescent tube is referred to as a gas discharge tube that generates visible light through fluorescence. It has a luminance efficiency of 45 to 100 lumen per watt. Fluorescent tubes consume less energy for the same amount of light than incandescent bulbs, although they are typically more complicated and expensive. Despite fluorescent lamps' poor color representation capabilities, these tubes offer a nice look and color. Many areas of a home can employ fluorescent tubes; however, dimmers cannot be used with them.

9. Light-Emitting Diode

A semiconductor device, such as an LED lamp, uses the movement of electrons to produce light. It has a long lifespan, requires less electricity, and does not have a filament. LEDs outperform incandescent bulbs in light output and contribute to energy-saving technologies. LEDs are often put together into a light bulb to be used as a LED lighting system. These diodes don't require color filters to output light of the desired color. A LED often has a high initial cost, yet these are used in electronic projects.

These kinds of lights or lamps are used in electrical application kits and lighting systems for indication purposes.

CHAPTER 8
ELECTRICAL GROUNDING

Applications for electrical wiring frequently call for grounding. For instance, the majority of cars and aircraft are built with grounding. It is a crucial safety feature that guards against arching, which might otherwise result in injury or fires.

8.1 Electrical Grounding

The process of generating an effective discharge path for electricity is known as electrical grounding. The reason it's called "grounding" is because the electricity is frequently directed to the ground, where it can discharge. Without grounding, electricity may build up to dangerously high levels inside wires or linked devices. The cables or gadgets may arc when this happens. This is avoided through grounding, ensuring that any excess voltage is safely released.

1. Working on Electrical Grounding

Utilizing the ground's negative electrical characteristics is how grounding operates. You are walking on a negatively electrically charged surface. As a result, it can cancel out electrical currents that are positively charged. Excess power can be discharged through the ground thanks to grounding. A grounding wire is present in most electrical systems. Automobile batteries, wiring for home appliances, and more contain grounding wires. The grounding wire is intended to be connected to the ground only. The ability of the ground to discharge more electricity is a result of its negative electrical characteristics.

Electricity is innately used to power electrical systems. However, as energy passes through them, it could accumulate in harmful amounts. Since they are grounded, most electrical systems are. The discharge of any extra power is guaranteed via grounding. The grounding wire that leads to the ground will be the path that the extra energy takes because it offers the least resistance. While there are various methods for grounding an electrical system, most involve connecting a grounding wire to either the earth or the chassis of a car or an airplane.

2. Why Do We Need Electrical Grounding Systems?

Grounded electrical systems are necessary for running a secure data center. They are, however, required for significant residential and commercial constructions. Grounding systems require sophisticated and time-consuming installation and maintenance, but they are necessary to avoid unsafe scenarios that could cause problems if an appliance inside wiring malfunctions. Using unground electrical systems carries several dangers, including the possibility of fire and electrical shocks, all of which can result in tragedies. The following are the benefits of using a properly grounded system:

I. Overload Protection

In an electrical workplace, excessive power surges can occur for many reasons, creating high electrical voltages in systems and resulting in fires and shocks that can seriously hurt or even kill people. By driving the extra surging energy into the ground, grounded systems provide overload protection for humans, electrical equipment, and any potentially important data they may contain.

II. Voltage Stabilization

To prevent circuits from being quickly overloaded and to evenly distribute power across different data sources, grounded systems are created. This ground provides a common reference point for essential voltage stabilization.

III. Protection From Electrical Hazards

In the worst case, ungrounding systems can result in shocks, fires, and equipment damage and destruction, which could cause major data loss and injury or death to people nearby. These electrical risks are eliminated by grounded systems, which shield the equipment from abrupt voltage surges, avert electrical fires, and lower the likelihood of harm to the equipment.

3. Types of Electrical Grounding

I. Ungrounded System

There is no direct link between the star point (neutral) and ground in ungrounded or unearthed systems. Since there are essentially no closed channels in these systems, the size of the ground faults is quite small. Theoretically, the conductors and ground have no potential, but AC systems always have capacitance between the conductors. We refer to these systems as being capacitively linked to the ground as a result. Ungrounded systems have an important characteristic in that it is highly challenging to locate the line-to-ground fault, even though the line-to-line ground fault currents are quite low.

II. Resistance Grounding

You may already know what this kind of grounding is. In resistive grounding, a resistor called a neutral earthing resistor is placed between the transformer's star point (neutral) and the ground. This resistor constrains the fault current that flows through the neutral conductor.

Low Resistance Grounding: The fault current in low resistance grounding is relatively significant, reaching up to 50A in some places. The value of the fault current varies from region to region.

High Resistance Grounding: The fault current in high resistance grounding is minimal, 10A or the current equal to the capacitive charging current.

III. Solidly Grounded Systems

The transformer's neutral (star point) is connected directly to the ground in systems that are either solidly grounded or directly grounded, with no additional resistance added to restrict current flow.

CHAPTER 9
ELECTRICAL DRAWING

9.1 Electrical Drawing

Electrical circuits are represented by lines, symbols, and numerical combinations in electrical diagrams and drawings used to illustrate electrical circuits. Electrical diagrams display the connections between components as well as their relative locations. We could better grasp the electrical circuits utilized in buildings with the aid of the electrical diagram. Electrical diagrams are used to complete the electrical wiring of a building, and electricians utilize these schematics to complete the electrical installation.

1. Why Is an Electrical Drawing Necessary?

Electrical drawings can be employed while creating new electrical systems, identifying electrical issues, and modifying an existing circuit. They are employed to diagnose issues and verify that all interconnections are made properly.

2. Types of Electrical Drawing

Different types of electrical drawings are discussed below.

I. Block Diagram

A block diagram depicts a system's main components or operations that connect the blocks to highlight their relationships.

II. Circuit Diagram

A simplified traditional graphical representation of an electrical circuit is a circuit drawing (diagram).

III. Pictorial Diagram

A pictorial diagram is a diagram that shows the components of a system using actual images or abstract, graphic graphics.

IV. Riser Diagram

The complete electrical circuit, from the service entry down to the smallest circuit branch, is shown on a riser diagram, which is a single-line diagram. It displays the diameter of the wire in each branch, the diameter of the conduit and the conductor at the service entrance, and the diameter of the protective device for the main breaker and each branch. It is called a riser diagram because it only depicts the routing of wiring or raceways from one level of the drawing to the next, not the positioning of the equipment in a particular room or space. These illustrations are employed because they are simple to understand.

V. Wiring Diagram

Symbols are used to represent the components of an electrically operated system on a wiring diagram. The lines represent the wires, and they are labeled with digits or letter-number pairings to show the connections between the different parts. The installation of cables in electrical equipment, such as switchboards and panels, is done by the device makers using wiring schematics. The connective cabling amongst the electrical equipment is displayed in the wiring diagram. These diagrams display the practical components in their proper spatial relationships. Lines show a single line with radial branches representing single conductors, multiple conductors installed in the same channel, and the conductor representation is identified by a number.

VI. Logic Diagram

It employs block type and standardized logic-function symbols to describe extremely complicated tasks that are carried out using two approaches: one is via individual devices while the second is via combining processing modules or by individual devices. It illustrates the reasoning for complex processes, circuits, or devices. Without a detailed understanding of the device's underlying processes, these diagrams will help users understand the relevant logic function. Complex functions are represented in these diagrams using blocks and symbols for the logic function; each block has a corresponding logic symbol. Signals used for process control follow a straight line. The input and output signals of the block are located at the sites where these signal routes enter and exit.

VII. Single-Line Diagram

It also goes by the name "one-line diagram," and it's primarily utilized in industrial power systems. The complicated power system is typically represented by a single-line diagram, which will show the electrical components and their connection. Problems with the electricity system can be identified using single-line diagrams. Finding out which circuit interrupters need to be activated to securely disconnect the electrical equipment can be helpful.

VIII. Elementary Drawings

These schematics will display every functional component as well as each circuit of a whole electrical control system. The full control circuit of an electrical substation is also represented by it.

IX. Three-Line Diagram

Three-line diagrams are employed to see comprehensive data about three-phase circuits that are not visible in a single-line diagram. These diagrams will be useful for plant upkeep and management staff, who can readily understand how the power system works. The components of the power system are depicted in the three-line diagrams using the same symbol as the single-line diagram. It also includes a few extra symbols common in wiring and schematic diagrams. These schematics will represent each conductor in an electrical circuit as a separate line.

X. Ladder Drawing

These drawings, which are specialized diagrams, are frequently used to describe manufacturing logic systems. The logic for system control is most frequently understood and designed using these diagrams. The ladder diagram is a top-downcast line schematic for logic function because it travels from a power input at the top through successive operations. Relay control circuits are illustrated using ladder diagrams. Compared to wiring diagrams, ladder diagrams are more conceptual and depict each branch of the circuit in its lateral row. These diagrams will explain how each branch works and how the operations arise from it. In a ladder diagram, the left vertical line is connected to the voltage source, while the right vertical line is linked to the ground. Each branch of the control circuit is represented by a set of horizontal rows in the vertical lines.

XI. Schematic Diagram

The schematic diagram demonstrates how the components of an electrical unit are connected using lines and symbols. Although the location of the parts is not indicated, we could make the electrical connections with the aid of this schematic. This schematic demonstrates the internal connections and circuit components in a configuration that enables an electrician to decipher an electrical control unit's operational logic and function. The symbols used in these diagrams can be seen in single-line, three-line, and wiring diagrams, which will display all terminals and connections of working devices. There are two further types of schematic diagrams.

External Schematic Drawing: These schematics will display the physical device's internal wiring as well as the external connections that carry signals throughout and out of the components.

Internal Schematic: Only the internal wiring of one specific physical device will be depicted in this drawing.

3. Reading of Electrical Drawings

Given below are some points that help in reading the electrical drawings:

I. Get to Know Standard Electrical Symbols

Understanding the meanings of the fundamental electrical symbols used in your electrical drawing will help you diagnose the circuit fast.

II. Acquire a Reading Style

Read schematics the same way you would a text document. Schematics should generally be read from top to bottom and left to right. The circuit will produce or use a signal that travels in this direction. To understand what the signal does or how it is transformed, the user can take the same route that the signal does.

III. Recognize Polarity

Certain circuit board components are polarized, which means that one edge is positive and the second is negative. It implies that there is a specific technique to which you must attach it. A symbol typically represents polarity. The usual rule of thumb is to determine which metal lead wire is longer to determine the physical component's polarity. The + side is the lengthier portion.

IV. Recognize Values and Names

Values aid in defining a component's identity. The value of an electrical component, such as a resistor, inductor, or capacitor, indicates how many ohms, farads, or Henries it has. The value can be the chip's name for other parts, such as integrated circuits. A schematic component's value identifies its most crucial feature.

Typically, component names are made up of a number and one or two letters. A component's type is indicated by the letter portion of its name, such as R for resistors, C for capacitors, U for integrated circuits, etc. Each element label in an electrical diagram needs to be distinct; for instance, if there are many resistors in a circuit, they should all be given the names R1, R2, R3, etc. The descriptive names of components make it easier to locate certain locations in diagrams. Name prefixes are generally standardized. The prefix for some components, such as resistors, is simply the component's first letter. Other name prefixes are not as literal; for instance, inductors are L's (since the current term has already taken I, yet it starts with a C; electronics is a funny field) rather than I's.

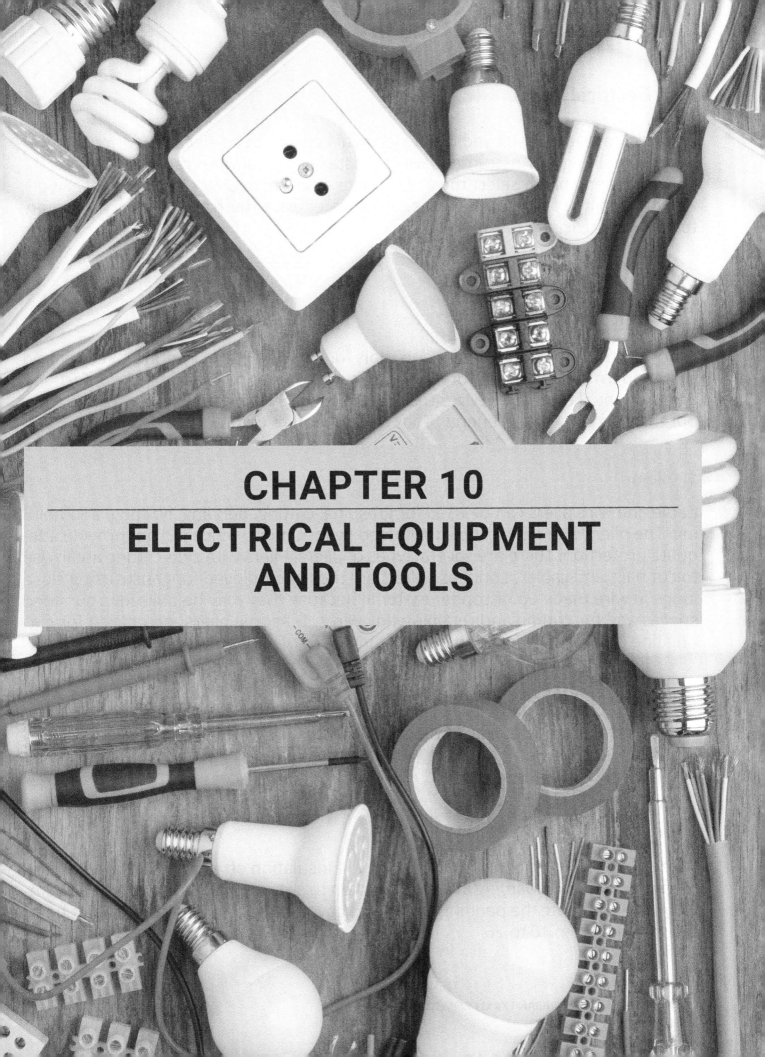

CHAPTER 10
ELECTRICAL EQUIPMENT AND TOOLS

10.1 Electrical Tools

Electrical tools are employed to do electrical tasks such as electrical wiring installations. By utilizing this instrument, we can install electrical wires rapidly and correctly. Only by being able to select the appropriate equipment or tools for electrical work will the quality of our job increase. Here we explain the hand, power, and safety tools the electrician uses.

10.2 Hand Tools

Every electrician requires basic hand tools for carrying out daily duties. Rees stated that modern basic models outperform their predecessors in terms of comfort and safety. Manual tools are devices that can be used or managed with our hands without the help of electrical energy. They do not require external power.

1. Pliers

Cable and wire pliers can be used for grasping, cutting, bending, twisting, and holding. The pliers' handles will be surrounded by insulation, which will not provide adequate protection. There are several types of pliers. Pliers with side-cutting are in use to cut nails and cables. Longnose pliers are mostly employed for constructing close loops in wire made up of copper material because they may be utilized in confined spaces and for cutting and retaining tiny wires. Diagonal pliers are utilized for cutting fine or medium wires and bending tiny faces of soft metal.

2. Wrenches

Wrenches may be used to hold stock or spin nuts while tightening bolts, nuts, and screws. There are several types of wrenches, such as adjustable and pipe wrenches and vice grip wrenches.

3. Wire Cutters

Wire strippers are employed for stripping the insulation off wires, most of which are medium-sized wires varying in gauge from ten to sixteen; wire strippers are also employed to amputate the padding from wires covered with rubber material that has a gauge range from 10 to 26.

4. Micrometer

A micrometer can be used to measure wires of various diameters, as well as to determine the diameter of circular wires. A micrometer can precisely measure the length of a tiny wire or the thickness of metal sheets.

5. Wire Diameter

Wire gauge is employed for determining the width or length of wires and the conductors' size. The wire gauge may be used to measure zero to thirty-six gauges.

6. Knife for Electricians

Linemen use these knives to cut the insulation off large cables in low-voltage and high-voltage transmission lines.

7. Multi-meter

A multimeter may be utilized to measure electrical current, voltage, frequency capacitance, resistance, and conductance; hence, one instrument can measure practically everything an electrician needs. This meter may also display the precise reading. There are both digital and analog multimeters on the market.

8. Screwdrivers

Screwdrivers are meant to tighten or loose the screws having slotted heads. The screwdrivers are available in various shapes and sizes depending upon the requirements of the user. Screwdrivers are constructed of steel and have a tempering tip. Different screwdrivers are used depending on the size and form of the screw.

9. Hacksaw

Hacksaws may be utilized for cutting insulated cable, metallic conduit, and medium- and small-sized metals.

10. Hammers

Hammers are instruments utilized for crushing and hammering out nails. They come in both hard and soft-faced varieties. A hard-faced hammer with a cylindrical head can strike hard items. The rewinding procedure is carried out with a soft-faced hammer. The majority of soft-faced hammers are constructed of rubber or plastic. Hammers come in various sizes and shapes, including claw hammers, ball peen hammers, and mallets.

10.3 Power Tools

Nowadays, power tools, whether corded or cordless, carry greater punch in smaller, lighter forms. The ergonomic design makes modern instruments more usable and less hazardous. Cordless power tools are gaining acceptance. Rees added that tool designs and recent advances in batteries and charging technology make them easier to use and adaptable, making workers more productive. Saws and drills, especially drills, are the most often utilized power tools for electricians.

1. Electric Drills

Electricians frequently install fresh lighting devices or deconstruct existing gear to gain access to wiring and other electric parts. A portable electric drill that includes multiple bits speeds up these processes while allowing experts to attach specialized drill bits, such as the reaming bit, for particular industry applications. When there is no electricity, electricians must rely on cordless drills.

2. Electric Tape

This pressure-sensitive adhesive substance is made of plastic, vinyl, or fiberglass fabric and is vital for insulation if wires or other substances carry electricity. This tape stops electrical current from going through other wires and electrocution when contacting live wires.

3. Cable Ties

These low-cost fasteners, sometimes called zip ties, are vital for connecting cables. Using cable ties, you can keep your electric space nice and organized.

4. Flashlights

Working in darkness poses a risk to an electrician. Keep necessary electrical tools, such as flashlights and other work lights, nearby and easily accessible.

5. Level

Finding exact placement places for light fixtures is critical when installing them. A standard level is essential for electricians to guarantee screws, fittings, and other installations are positioned exactly where they need to be.

6. Connector for Splicing

These plastic clips aid electricians in making rapid connections with several wires. They are compatible with various cables, comprising electric cables, device wires, and telephone cables.

7. Lugs for Wires and Cables

Cable and wire lugs, similar to those seen on jumper cables and automobile batteries, join wires to equipment, cables, and other devices that require electricity.

8. Conduit Bender

Electricians frequently run wiring around the corner of a wall or in other generally hidden regions while establishing a wiring path. Conduit benders are tools for electricians employed to bend conduit pipes to fit these paths while also ensuring that the conduits are nonintrusive and effectively positioned in the customer's home.

9. Coax Connector

Coax connectors link cables with devices and shield the cable from shred. There are several connections available, and maintaining a selection on hand ensures that you constantly satisfy your client's demands.

10. Reaming Tool

Establishing new conduits or restoring old ones entails joining various sections of piping to form a wire path between the electrical parts. A reaming bit, attached to an electric drill, expands the aperture on one end of the pipe, allowing it to connect to another piping segment and complete a secure conduit.

11. Fish Tape

One of the most used electrician tools is fish tape. It is employed to connect gang boxes or related electric equipment through conduit pipes. The fish tape is enclosed in a flexible coil and may be fed via a conduit pipe that has been constructed. When the end of the fish tape is visible on the other side, the wiring may be attached to it, and the tape retracted, drawing the wire along the conduit.

12. Terminal Block

These insulated, modular devices aid electricians in combining several wires. They connect the wire to the ground or connect electrical switches and outlets to power sources.

13. Fishing Rods

Fishing rods are important electrician equipment when putting wire into walls, above carpets, and ceilings. Rods are normally made of fiberglass and have hooks on the end for easy maneuverability.

10.4 Electrician Safety Equipment

1. Insulated Gloves

Electricians are at risk of electrocution and must take safeguards. Wearing insulated gloves adds an extra layer of protection from shocks caused by electricity, so keep them on hand as part of your electrical repair kit. Insulated gloves are available in various designs for comfort and fit; select the one that works most effectively for you.

2. Hook/Rescue Rod

Hook or Rescue rods are employed for removing heavy objects or unconscious persons who have been shocked from a potentially dangerous area. Because a harmful current of electricity may still be present, emergency personnel have to employ the rescue rod to remove a victim from the source of power without becoming electrocuted.

3. Safety Glasses

You must wear eye protection when carefully inspecting electrical wiring, operating power tools, electricians, or cutting wires. Apprentices and seasoned veterans require a pair of safety glasses on every job site as part of their necessary electrician gear.

4. Fire-Resistant Work Shirt

Experienced and certified electricians understand how to avoid hazardous electrocutions and fires. As part of this education, they must wear working shirts made of fire-resistant material to avoid major injuries from burns.

5. Head Protection

Power workers or Electricians are frequently required to climb ladders and even greater heights to perform maintenance and inspect wiring and power lines. Appropriate head protection is essential for lowering the risk of deadly falls. Electrical workers' hard helmets will satisfy the ANSI Class E standard. According to the specification, these hard helmets protect against falling objects and limit the danger of burns up to 20,000 volts and high-voltage electrical shocks.

The Ridgeline XR7 helmet, which was just released, is intended for employees who spend a lot of time up there. It not only complies with ANSI Class E but also with some additional safety requirements. Full Brim hard and Non-vented Ridgeline Cap Style helmets, SL Series Cap Style and Full Brim hard hats, and select SL Series Sleek Shell choices are also Class E compliant. Dielectric adapters are also available for head protection. This enables employees to customize their hard helmets with extras such as earmuffs and face shields. During the COVID-19 outbreak, adapters were especially helpful for adding face coverings for employees without interfering with correct PPE wear.

10.5 Other Electrical Safety Devices

Hearing protection and high-visibility clothing is not usually required when working with electricity. Most headphones and earplugs are excellent choices for electrical safety equipment. However, metal-detecting earbuds should be ignored. Electrical and power employees on work sites near highways should wear high-visibility clothes to be seen in vehicles. While adequate PPE is essential for electricians and power workers, voltage testers, safety tools, insulated tools, harnesses, and voltage testers should also be incorporated into an electrical safety toolbox.

CHAPTER 11
ELECTRICAL MAINTENANCE AND TROUBLESHOOTING

11.1 What is Troubleshooting?

Troubleshooting is the procedure of finding faults with malfunctioning equipment and implementing remedial procedures to restore it to peak performance. Technicians do this by separately or together evaluating the different components to isolate defects that arise when using the product in issue.

11.2 What Causes Electrical Equipment Failures?

Determining the most likely reasons for the problem is a good place to start troubleshooting defective equipment. Equipment failures may be categorized into functional failures and failures caused by operating circumstances. There are several examples of the latter, some of which are discussed below.

1. Temperature/Heating Excess

High ambient temperatures, except for heat-resistant components, can be damaging to different parts of a circuit. Overheating can occur in some devices when the main cooling mechanism fails (for example, a laptop's functioning heat sink and cooling fan).

2. Failure Patterns

Failures may happen between starting and completing an electrical product's useful life. The mode of failure relates to the number of operational breakdowns that a device may present, which is normally restricted. The following are examples of common issues:

A. Corrosion failure

The corrosion failure includes corrosion and deposits of minerals that occur on metallic terminals or connections.

B. Mechanical failures

This type of failure involves shattered components, broken electromechanical connections because of severe mechanical stress, and so on.

3. Extensive Use

Electrical machinery that is heavily used, particularly over its intended lifetime, will ultimately have defective components. Furthermore, numerous gadgets that have long been relied on in industrial conditions with high temperatures and vibration will eventually give way to internal component damage caused by mechanical and overheating trauma.

4. Overvoltage and Overcurrent

Overcurrent happens when the electrical current flowing across a conductor exceeds its highest-rated current. Ground faults, short circuits, and overloading are all common causes. Overvoltage happens when the voltage inside an electrical part surpasses its highest-rated voltage, similar to the overcurrent. For example, if 220V to 240V-rated equipment gets 350V from an electrical supply, it is overvoltage.

Electric arcs, power surges, and poor insulation are frequent causes of overvoltage. The installed insulation fails when the voltage supply is far higher than the highest working voltage, allowing some current to flow through.

5. Short Circuits

Bridged connections caused by humidity, deteriorated insulation, and corrosion, can allow increased current flow across electric circuits, eventually resulting in a short circuit. Overheating caused by short-circuiting can result in explosions or electrical fires.

11.3 Techniques for Troubleshooting Electrical Equipment

Electric circuits are made up of separate components that might fail when a product nears the end of its lifespan. The strategies listed below can help you solve difficulties and get your device back up and running.

1. Conductor Troubleshooting

A multimeter's continuity feature can be utilized to check the connected wires' status. When the multimeter's probes are linked between any two lengths of wire, it will emit a beeping sound and indicate infinite resistance (the OL that is an Open-Loop measurement). Such signs imply the usage of a good conductor.

2. Physical Examination

A thorough physical examination of electrical equipment is required to detect corrosion, faults, chips, cracks, and other types of harm to its internal parts. To standardize the approach, engineers frequently verify items against a checklist. Engineers can also use visual examination to detect bridging connections, break-down insulation, loose electrical wiring, and worn electromechanical contacts, among other issues, which can lead to open or short circuits and other issues.

3. Signal Analysis

To verify the behavior of digital circuits, oscilloscopes, and logical analyzers are utilized. These components generate circuit parameter data and graphically show it on the user interface. This type of output data may be utilized to pinpoint flaws in an electric circuit.

4. Passive Component Testing

The behavior of electric circuits is controlled by passive components like diodes, resistors, and capacitors. Faulty or damaged components can cause several failure states. Technicians can use a multimeter to test and isolate defective passive components, which can be examined while still connected to the rest of the circuit.

5. Functional Areas Testing

Electrical components comprise numerous functional regions, including processors, power supplies, and signal lines. Engineers enhance fault detection accuracy by evaluating functional sections individually. Parts with faulty components should be separated promptly.

6. Circuit Protection Device Testing

During abnormal situations, blown fuses, faulty relays, or tripped circuits, breakers assist in isolating electrical equipment from a power supply. One or more circuit protection devices may have failed, resulting in an appliance that will not switch on. By checking for continuity between the terminals, multimeters may detect blown fuses. It should be noted that relays and breakers should be reset to their ON/closed states before using the multimeter to check for continuity.

11.4 Hardware Troubleshooting Tools Electricians Need

Electronic hardware troubleshooting tools are generally testing equipment for circuit characteristics and signals.

1. Digital Multimeters

Multimeters are an extremely important component of testing equipment. They may check circuit characteristics, including resistance, current, and voltage. Multimeters may also evaluate voltages of up to 50VDC and 250VAC. It should be noted that currents ranging from 250mA - 10A are appropriate for diagnosing most circuits.

2. Documentation

The manufacturer's product documentation is crucial for proper troubleshooting. Diagrams of power distribution, Circuit diagrams, part numbers (for replacing defective components), and even diagnostic software are illustrations.

3. Logic Analyzer

Several signals from digital circuitry are captured and shown using a logic analyzer. The output can detect faults (such as during integrated circuit testing).

4. Oscilloscope

An electronic test device known as an oscilloscope is used to physically examine and interpret waveforms produced by electric circuits. Technicians can more readily pinpoint problematic areas of devices owing to such produced output.

11.5 Troubleshooting and Maintenance of Advanced Electrical Equipment and Systems

As a facilities technician, you ensure the safe and effective operation of electrical equipment and systems in complex facilities, including data centers, hospitals, industries, and airports. The criteria of Electrical engineering and NEC must be followed; however, they are insufficient to avoid or remedy issues caused by aging, damage, environmental variables, or human mistake. Here we will teach you how to use a systematic approach and some practical techniques to repair and maintain electrical equipment and systems in complicated facilities.

1. Determine the Issue

The initial phase in troubleshooting is determining the nature of the problem. You must collect data from various sources, including alerts, reports, records, sensors, meters, and visual inspections. You should also interview affected or involved users, operators, or maintenance personnel. Some questions to consider include: What is the symptom? How frequently does it happen? When did it all begin? What may be the probable causes? What are the ramifications? What are the applicable rules and regulations?

2. Determine the Root Reason

The following step is to identify the source of the issue by evaluating, determining, or analyzing the electrical tools and systems. You will need to employ instruments like multimeters, power analyzers, oscilloscopes, and circuit testers. You must also follow safety protocols and safeguards, which include donning protective equipment, shutting out and tagging out, and de-energizing the circuits. You can use the following methods: Examine the stability, the current, the voltage, resistance, and power. Check the results against the specifications, instructions, or diagrams. Identify the circuits or components that connect the source to the load. Examine the system for evidence of harm, loose connection, corrosion, or overheating.

3. Put the Solution into Action

The third phase is to implement the issue solution by fixing, replacing, or changing electrical systems and equipment. Cables, equipment connections, fuses, switches that operate, and soldering irons are examples of materials, parts, or equipment that must be used. You must also adhere to high standards and best practices, which include matching ratings, colors, or sizes. You can do the following steps: Reconnect the terminals, cables, or components, then tighten or clean them. Replace any worn-out or damaged components, which include fuses, relays, breakers, and capacitors. Change the voltage, speed, and frequency parameters.

4. Check the Results

The fourth stage is testing, measuring, or observing the electrical devices and systems to ensure the solution's findings are correct. Identical methods and instruments must be used in the isolation stage. You must also adhere to the reporting and documentation requirements, such as capturing data, maintaining logs, and filling out forms. You can look for the following indicators: The symptoms have disappeared or have been lessened; the measurements are within the acceptable range; and the device or system's operation is correct or effective.

5. Avoid Recurrence

The final step is to keep the problem from recurring through periodic checks and maintenance on electrical devices and systems. You must adhere to the preventative maintenance plan and checklist, which might be monthly, quarterly, or annually. You must also follow the ideas for enhancement and innovation, which include updating, installing, and retrofitting new features. You can complete the following tasks: Clean, calibrate, or lubricate the entire system or equipment. Replace any filters, batteries, or bulbs that have failed. Surge protectors, grounding rods, and backup generators should all be installed.

6. Discover and Share

The sixth stage is to analyze the procedure and results to learn and share from the troubleshooting experience. You must determine the lessons learned and best practices, especially what worked well, what did not, what may be improved, and what should be avoided. You must also share your expertise and comments with your coworkers, bosses, or clients, for example, through presentations, newspapers, and newsletters. You can obtain the following advantages: Improve your abilities and self-esteem; build your confidence and reputation; and improve your interaction and cooperation.

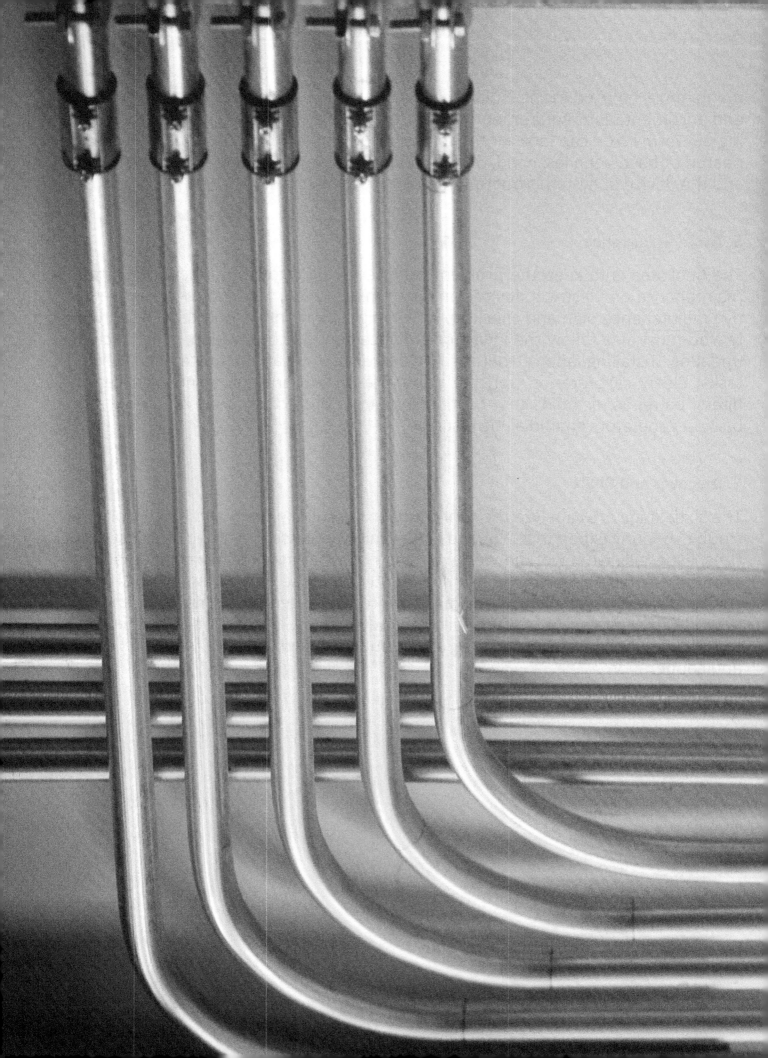

CHAPTER 12
CONDUIT BENDING AND INSTALLATION

12.1 Electrical Conduit

A raceway used to store and protect electrical cables within a structure or building is known as an electrical conduit. Electrical conduits are essential to the modern world, from data centers to subterranean subways to ports and bridges. Several varieties are available depending on the use. According to the demands of the installation environment, the conduit selected for your project may be rigid or flexible. It may provide various degrees of protection from impact, gases, corrosion, vapors, moisture, fire, and electromagnetic interference. Wet, extremely corrosive, or dangerous environments generally need specialist conduits.

According to the NEC (National Electrical Code), the electrical conduit may also be approved for direct enclosure with concrete, that's typical in commercial uses. The capacity to field bend conduit and its permitted supporting spacings will influence the number of fittings (couplings, connectors, elbows) required for a project and its cost. Conduit bodies are used by electricians to connect separate portions of a conduit. A conduit body has a detachable cover that allows simple access to the cables. You may reverse the polarity of cables to protect your electrical system.

12.2 What Materials Are Used to Make Conduit Bodies?

A conduit body is made out of copper-free aluminum gaskets and coverings. The aluminum protects the metal bolts from water and corrosion. They are made of lightweight, corrosion-resistant material. Conduit boxes are also resistant to moisture, so they may be used outside in rain and snow. Devices with an epoxy powder coating are more resistant to corrosion. To meet your electrical preferences, you might remove the neoprene gasket. Conduit bodies might be used for IMC, EMT, rigid, threaded, or a mix of wiring. The number of wires that may be accommodated in the conduit is determined by the various diameters and forms.

12.3 Types of Electrical Conduits

Different types of metallic and non-metallic electrical conduits are explained below.

1. Metal Electrical Conduits

I. Intermediate Metal Conduit (IMC)

An intermediate metal conduit (IMC) is a steel conduit rated for outdoor usage, somewhat lighter than RMC, and approved for the same purposes as RMC. It is available threaded or unthreaded, can be more affordable than RMC, and may or may not be coated. IMC has substantially thinner walls than GRC and RMC, which allows it to support more wire fill but makes it more prone to kinking. IMC is much smaller than other conduits since its trade sizes only go up to 4 inches.

II. Rigid Metal Conduit (RMC)

RMC is made of heavyweight galvanized steel and is fitted with threaded fittings. It is well-known for its strength, but it is also one of the more expensive electrical conduits in terms of both materials and labor. Aluminum is another RMC material that may have an extra coating added to improve corrosion resistance.

III. Electrical Metallic Tubing (EMT)

A metallic electrical tubing (EMT) is a thin-walled, unthreaded material that frequently replaces GRC in commercial and industrial settings. It is also frequently utilized in residential settings. It can also be constructed of aluminum and is authorized for use in concrete; however, it cannot be put in areas that might be damaged physically. EMT cannot provide the same level of security as GRC can. It is bent easily despite being thin but cannot be field threaded. The typical trade sizes vary from 0.5 inches to 1.5 inches.

IV. Galvanized Rigid Steel (GRC)

Galvanized Rigid Steel (GRC) is a steel product approved for use in both indoor and outdoor settings. It is incorporated in commercial and industrial settings and provides UV stability, impressive impact resistance, and EMI (electromagnetic interference) protection. GRC is a long-standing industry standard. Unfortunately, GRC is extremely costly to install and may be very corrosive because of its enormous weight and poor field handling. GRC is prone to a fault when the conduit and wire may solder together because of their conductivity.

2. Non-Metallic Electrical Conduits

I. Electrical Nonmetallic Tube (ENT)

Although ENT (Electrical Nonmetallic Tube) has a thin wall and is corrugated, it is not fire rated. Although it is frequently employed inside walls or within concrete blocks, it is not permitted in open situations. ENT, which is renowned for its remarkable flexibility, may be manually bent in the field without the use of any special equipment or heat. PVC is offered in trade sizes up to 2 inches for ENT. Three feet is the maximum support spacing, and terminations must be three feet apart.

II. RTRC Conduit

RTRC conduits exist in a variety of forms depending on their threading and wall thickness. RTRC is made from a material called fiberglass by rotating the strands over the blade via a tension-winding technique. Later, the fibers are impregnated with resin followed by treatment at a high temperature which produces the strands having increased flexibility and temperature resistance. RTRC has the greatest variety of corrosion resistance of any conduit substance on the market, as well as reduced burn-through, UV stability, exceptional temperature range (including outstanding low-temperature handling), and the ability to keep its original form after impact. It has equivalent support distances to PVC-coated steel, GRC, and aluminum electrical conduit.

According to the NECA (National Electrical Contractors Association) Manual of Labor Units, RTRC is much lighter than typical conduit materials, resulting in the lowest labor installation rates for most diameters. It is one of the cheapest electrical conduit solutions in terms of raw material costs. Phenolic RTRC complies with NFPA 130 and is appropriate for specialty applications needing no flame, low smoke, zero halogens, and a 2-hour fire-rated conduit for Class I Div 2 environments.

III. PVC Conduit

PVC conduits are manufactured and exist in different forms depending on their threads and wall thickness. PVC is lightweight and frequently utilized for electrical conduit applications made of non-electrical material. Due to its low UV resilience, PVC conduit is not advised for use in direct sunlight. With the use of a hotbox conduit bender, it is very simple to heat and field bend. Still, due to a high coefficient of thermal expansion, it must be placed to allow for expansion and contraction and may distort after installation in overly hot situations. PVC was formerly a cheap conduit, but due to persistent supply chain problems, it has recently become more expensive and difficult to get. When this occurs, RTRC produced in America is frequently used.

IV. Rigid Nonmetallic Conduit (RNC)

Smooth-walled, non-metallic, unthreaded tubing is offered in various materials, such as PVC, polyethylene with a high density, and RTRC (fiberglass). Several types of RNC are permitted for use underground or in direct burial, albeit the specifications and capabilities differ according to the substrate.

3. Purpose of Conduit Body

One of the most adaptable components of electrical raceways is conduit bodies. The raceway system, which is attached to the conduit, includes a conduit body. Through conduit fittings, conduits are connected to the conduit body. Take into consideration that:

- You need taps for the conduit branches.
- Pull outlets should be provided for installed conductors.
- Wires should be accessible for future maintenance and replacement requirements.
- You should make tap and splice conductor holes.
- Conduit runs should be able to bend 90 degrees.
- Conduit wiring parts should be combined.

Threaded wires or EMT conduits are supported by IMC conduit bodies. To accommodate threaded adapters, non-metallic conduit bodies connect to PVC conduits. Conduit bodies are used by electricians to store wire or splicing equipment. They can also be utilized as junctions or pull boxes. Pulling access to a run of conduits is made possible by conduit bodies. To save space, conduit bodies can be bent. They might be used to divide a conduit passage into many directions.

4. What Advantages Do Conduit Bodies Offer?

One of the many methods to connect conduits is via a conduit body. You may reach the interior of the raceway to pull, check, and maintain electrical wires through the conduit body. Your system can operate well when you have more control over your wiring. They may also assist in changing the direction of your wires' power or bend them in a certain direction. Conduit bodies are another option for splicing wires. Connecting two wires to increase their current carrying capacity is known as wire splicing. Always, a conduit comes to an end at a box-shaped piece of equipment, such as an electric box. Conduit bodies and the conduit can be joined using specialized fittings. The conduit wires, box, and connections make up the raceway. Depending on the kind of conduit, conduit bodies should be connected. Connect a metal conduit to metal boxes and a plastic conduit to plastic boxes.

Our fittings are simple to install while offering your electrical raceways more fire resistance. In the event of a fire, they may also extinguish themselves. Find the best material for your conduit system by perusing our selection of conduit fittings.

5. A Guide to Electrical Conduit Selection

Which conduit should be considered for usage in a project is often determined by technical requirements, local codes, and National Electrical Code (NEC) recommendations. When choosing an electrical conduit, several factors must be taken into account in addition to size and type, such as:

- Cable issue
- Wage costs
- Toxicity
- Memory for field handling
- Weight
- Material expense
- Durability
- Separating expansion joints
- Range of temperatures
- Conductivity
- Suspension spans
- Friction coefficient
- Burn-through

The ideal conduit ought to:

- Keep costs low.
- Be strong and enduring.
- Allow for the easy pulling of cables to locations that could become inaccessible in the future.
- Be resistant to pulling lubricants and with little to no burn-through.
- Be fire-resistant, as required by the environment or application.

6. Conduit Body Installation Guide

You will need assistance from another individual to install conduit bodies. The trainer will be one person, and the puller will be other one. Wires are fed through the conduit body's access point by the trainer and pulled out to the other end by the assistant.

I. Organize the wiring in groups

Before attaching the wires to the instrument, place them in the conduit, and group the wiring collectively rather than clumping it. Connect the wires that must pass through the conduit body using fish tape.

II. Wires being bent

Within the conduit body, make a pulling loop. The maximum bend that may be made between any two pull points is 360 degrees. The insulation might be harmed by doing this. Instead, put more work into running your conduit straight.

III. Through the conduit, push the wiring

To prevent the wires from rubbing against the hub, use lubrication. So that you don't restrict the cables, slowly push the wire through.

CHAPTER 13
PRACTICE TEST

Practice Test 1

1. During no load conditions, an induction motor will have a P.F_____.

A) 0.7
B) 0.5
C) 0.2
D) 0.9

Answer: C

Explanation: Because of the high magnetizing current, the induction motor's power factor is low when there is no load.

2. A general representation of motor load is_____.

A) Both resistance and inductance
B) Combination of Resistance, Inductance, and Capacitance
C) Resistance alone
D) Inductance alone

Answer: A

Explanation: An electrical motor's winding is made up of inductors and resistance.

3. In iron cores, __ are inefficient circulation currents that cause energy loss.

A) Core Currents
B) Eddy Currents
C) Both Hysteresis and Eddy Currents
D) Hysteresis Currents

Answer: B

Explanation: Circulating currents called eddy currents are produced in the core and serve no purpose. Eddy currents will cause I2R losses. Therefore, when magnetic fields in a conductor or core fluctuate, eddy current losses are produced.

4. _____ devices have the highest efficiency?

A) D.C. Motor
B) Induction motor
C) Synchronous machine
D) Electrical Transformer

Answer: D

Explanation: Transformer won't have moving components like other electrical devices, and the flux route won't have an air gap.

5. A self-starting motor is a single-phase induction motor:

A) True
B) False

Answer: B

Explanation: Due to its inability to generate a revolving magnetic field like a three-phase induction motor, single-phase induction motors are not self-stating.

6. It is impossible to minimize the effect of electrostatic charge on a body's surface by connecting it to the ground.

A) True
B) False

Answer: B

Explanation: An electrostatic charge dissipates to the ground when it is connected to the ground.

7. When a nonlinear load is coupled to the supply system, non-sinusoidal voltage and current waveforms are produced:

A) False
B) True

Answer: B

Explanation: When non-linear loads like computers and televisions are connected to the supply system, the voltage and current passing through the system will be distorted, which leads to the generation of harmonics.

8. The basis for how an electrical generator operates is _____:

A) Maxwell's law
B) Fleming's left-hand rule
C) Amperes rule
D) Fleming's Right-hand rule

Answer: D

Explanation: Electrical generators operate according to Fleming's Right Hand Rule.

9. Three resistances of 3 ohms each wired in parallel will have the _____ comparable resistance:

A) 1.5 Ω
B) 1 Ω
C) 9 Ω
D) 4.5 Ω

Answer: B

Explanation: In parallel resistance, as per the formula below

=

Ω

10. The operating resistance of a 40 W, 240V tungsten light is:

A) 1400 Ohms
B) 1440 Ohms
C) 1250 Ohms
D) 1380 Ohms

Answer: B

Explanation: $R = V^2/P = (240)^2/40 = 1440$ Ohms

Practice Test 2

1. How efficient is a 10-hp motor if it uses 40 amps at 240V?

A) 86.1 %
B) 96.5%
C) 77.7 %
D) 97.1%

Answer: C

Explanation: As we know that

P in = V.I=240*40=9600W

Efficiency= output power*746/input power= (10*746)/9600=0.777

2. Voltage waveforms in circuits powering capacitive loads will lag behind current waveforms:

A) False
B) True

Answer: B

Explanation: The voltage waveform in a capacitor circuit trails the current waveform and has a higher power factor. The exact opposite will occur in an inductive circuit.

3. A parallel of four 1-ohm resistances connects in series with a 5-ohm resistance. Find the circuit's equivalent resistance to be.

A) 4.75 ohms
B) 5.25 ohms

Answer: B

Explanation: 5.25 ohms are equal to 5 ohms in series with 4 parallel circuits of 1 ohm each.

4. Which of the following quantity is the same in a series electrical circuit:

A) Electrical Current
B) Electrical Voltage
C) Electrical Resistance
D) Electrical Power

Answer: A

Explanation: In a series circuit, the amount of current flowing through the circuit won't change.

5. When used in electrical transformers, transformer oil:

A) Insulating material
B) It depends on the application of the transformer
C) Coolant
D) Both Insulating material and coolant

Answer: D

Explanation: Transformer oil serves as a coolant and an insulation medium in an electrical transformer.

6. A lamp powered by 120V has a 10 resistance. What is the lamp's power?

A) 1 kW
B) 1.44 kW

Answer: B

Watts = P = V2/R = (120)2/10=1440KW

1. What substance is in the fuse:

A) Copper
B) Lead
C) Tin
D) Iron

Answer: C

Explanation: The fuse is made up of tin.

7. **A 60 Hz A.C. circuit has a voltage of 120 volts and a current of 12 amps; the current is 60 degrees behind the voltage. To convert power to watts:**

A) 720 watts
B) 850 watts

Answer: A

Explanation: 720 watts are equal to P = V * I * Cos (phi) or 120 * 12 * 1/2.

8. **Using a Wattmeter, you may quantify power in:**

A) D.C. circuits only
B) A.C. circuits only
C) Both AC and D.C. circuits
D) None of the above circuits

Answer: C

Explanation: Wattmeter is utilized to measure both ac and dc power.

9. **Which of the items listed below is measured with a megger?**

A) Voltage
B) Ampere-hour
C) Power factor
D) Resistance

Answer: D

Explanation: Meggar is utilized for the measurement of the insulation resistance.

Practice Test 3

1. **The mineral-insulated cables' PVC covering serves as protection from the following:**

A) Corrosion
B) Electric shock
C) Lighting
D) Sunlight

Answer: A

Explanation: To aid in identification and to offer an extra layer of corrosion protection, a colored plastic sheath may be placed over the metal sheath in mineral-insulated cables.

2. _____tests must be performed to acquire direct measurements of the motor's output and efficiency.

A) Speed test
B) Friction test
C) Performance test
D) Brake test

Answer: D

Explanation: Due to the situation with huge engines. The brake produces a lot of heat that is hard to release. Both a belt brake and a rope brake can be used to perform the load test.

3. The electromagnet's core is constructed of _____:

A) Cobalt steel
B) Alnico
C) Carbon steel
D) Soft iron

Answer: D

Explanation: The electromagnet core is soft iron because of its low retentivity and high sensitivity.

4. Cable insulation composed of PVC is indicated by the acronym:

A) Polyvinyl Compound
B) Polyvinyl Chloroprene
C) Polyvinyl Covering
D) Polyvinyl Chloride

Answer: D

Explanation: It allows cables to withstand abrasion, U.V., heat, oils, acids, and alkalis.

5. The machine is cooled using hydrogen cooling in massive synchronous generators:

A) False
B) True

Answer: B

6. The load on the secondary side of an instrument transformer is referred to as

A) Rating
B) Burden
C) Capacity
D) Output

Answer: B

Explanation: The main load source in a current transformer electrical network is the secondary winding's resistive resistance.

7. The twisted result of a motor's shaft is known as:

A) Torque
B) Inertia
C) Acceleration
D) Momentum

Answer: A

Explanation: A shaft develops shear stress when a bending moment or a torque is put on it.

8. Power loss in an electrical machine brought on by regular magnetic reversals causes:

A) Copper loss
B) Hysteresis loss
C) Friction loss
D) Eddy current loss

Answer: B

Explanation: The magnetic instability of the iron's molecules and their reluctance to move cause hysteresis losses.

9. _____ is true if the transformer's transformation ratio is specified as 10:1?

A) There is one secondary turn for every ten main turns in the transformer.
B) It is a step-up transformer.
C) There is one main turn for every ten secondary turns on the transformer's secondary side.

Answer: A

Explanation: This indicates that just 1050 V is being applied as the terminal voltage to the transformer's primary. The secondary voltage of the transformer is 105 V with a 10:1 turn ratio.

10. The useful power output to total power input ratio is __.

A) Work done
B) Diversity factor
C) Efficiency
D) Power factor

Answer: C

Explanation: Efficiency is the measure of a machine's energy input to energy output ratio.

Practice Test 4

1. One conduit can hold two or more cables, which is referred to as____:

A) Bunched
B) Shared
C) Grouped
D) Phase

Answer: A

Explanation: Listed are the conductor size and quantity restrictions permitted by NEC Code 300.17: No over fifty-three percent of a conduit can be filled by one wire. No over thirty percent of a conduit can be filled by two wires. No over forty percent of a conduit can be filled with three or more wires.

2. A five-horsepower motor has a power output of _____ Watts.

A) 7460 watts
B) 3000 watts
C) 3730 watts
D) 746 watts

Answer: C

Explanation: 1 HP = 746 Watts

5 HP = 5*746 = 3730 Watts

3. The letters "n" and "p" that come before a semi-conducting diode stand for:

A) Pat number reference
B) Material doping process.
C) Phase and neutral mode
D) Phase sequence rotation

Answer: B

Explanation: Since the cathode (n-type material) is where electrons come from, it is represented by the vertical bar. Since the anode (p-type material) is where the electrons travel, an arrow is used to depict it.

4. The efficiency of thermal power plants will be in the _____ range:

A) 70 to 80%
B) 50 to 60%
C) Above 80%
D) 30 to 40%

Answer: D

Explanation: The proportion of the thermal equivalent of mechanical energy delivered to the shaft of the turbine and the heat of combustion is known as the thermal efficiency of a steam power plant.

5. _____ quantities are measured by a pyrometer?

A) Magnetic moments
B) Temperature
C) The density of the materials
D) Electrical Flux

Answer: B

Explanation: For the measurement of extremely high temperatures, pyrometers are employed.

6. To lower the resistance of the grounded or the earthing process system, naphthalene is used:

A) False
B) True

Answer: B

7. _____ are two electrodes utilized in the manufacture of lead-acid cells:

A) Lead and Lead monoxide
B) Lead and Lead peroxide
C) Lead and Lead oxide
D) Lead and Lead sulfate

Answer: C

Explanation: The negative electrode of a lead acid battery is formed of porous or spongy lead. Because lead is permeable, it may dissolve and develop more easily. Lead oxide makes up the positive electrode.

8. A primary cell's zinc plate corrosion is referred to as _____:

A) Polarization
B) Local action
C) Amalgamation
D) Ionization

Answer: B

Explanation: The degradation of a battery caused by currents moving to and from another electrode is known as local action.

9. The power dissipated when a 10-ohm resistor is subjected to a 5-amp current is:

A) 400 watts
B) 250 watts
C) 350 watts
D) 500 watts

Answer: B

Explanation: $P = I^2 R$

P= 5*5*10=250 watts

10. A body's motion-induced energy is made up of_____:

A) Kinetic energy
B) Thermal energy
C) Electrical energy
D) Potential energy

Answer: A

Explanation: The energy of a moving body, or kinetic energy, corresponds to the kinetic energy of all things in motion.

Practice test 5

1. The fundamental S.I. length unit is____:

A) Km
B) cm
C) mm
D) m

Answer: D

Explanation: Length is typically measured in meters.

2. What is the sum of the capacitance for 5 parallel-connected capacitors with ratings of 10, 20, 30, 40, and 50 microfarads, respectively?

A) 120 microfarads
B) 150 microfarads

Answer: B

Explanation: $C_{eq} = C_1 + C_2 + C_3 + C_3 + C_4 + C_5 = 10+20+30+40+50 = 150$

3. Two resistors are connected in a parallel connection of 20 and 1 ohms; find the resistance equivalent.

A) 6.67 ohm
B) 6.5 ohm

Answer: A

Explanation: = 1/20+1/1= 6.67

4. _____ is reduced by the lamination of the transformer?

A) Flux leakage losses
B) Noise
C) Iron losses
D) Weight

Answer: C

Explanation: Each component's area is lowered by including laminations, resulting in an extremely high resistance that restricts the eddy current to a low value and lowers eddy current losses.

5. ____ measures speed while illuminating at a predetermined frequency is known as

A) Oscilloscope
B) Light meter
C) Stroboscope
D) Pulse meter

Answer: C

Explanation: The contact speed of the stroboscope may be measured. The stroboscope's measuring range for contact frequency measurements is 0.5 to 99,999 RPM. Along with the contact information

6. _____ exhibits the skin effect phenomenon:

A) In both D.C and A.C circuits
B) Only in EHV circuits
C) A.C. circuits
D) D.C. circuits

Answer: C

Explanation: As it is the propensity of alternating currents with high frequencies to accumulate near a conducting material's surface

7. A 3-phase induction motor's two phases can be reversed to provide the _____ effects:

A) The motor will rotate.
B) No change will take place.
C) The motor rotates in the opposite direction.
D) It should not be done as it is dangerous to the motor.

Answer: C

Explanation: Motors with three phases gyrate in the magnetic field's direction of rotation. These motors' rotational axes may be simply adjusted. Two of the power lines' connections to the motor leads are switched around to achieve this.

8. _____ characteristics should be present in an electrical transformer core:

A) Low permittivity
B) High Permeability
C) High permittivity
D) Low permeability

Answer: B

Explanation: Permeability is the term used to describe a material's capacity to transport magnetic flux. And compared to air, iron or steel has a lot better ability. The majority of transformer components are built with extremely high permeabilities.

9. A material needs the following to act like an excellent conductor:

A) An electron in the outermost orbital
B) Electron does not decide the material conductivity property.
C) Pair of electrons in the outer orbital
D) More than 2 electrons in the outer orbital

Answer: A

Explanation: The electrons in the outermost orbit may flow freely within the lattice that makes up Meta's physical structure because of this.

10. At 120V, an electric iron consumes 10 amps. How much electricity does the electric iron use:

A) 1.2 kW
B) 1.4 kW

Answer: A

Explanation: P=I*V= 10*120=1200watts or 1.2 KW

Practice Test 6

1. _____ must be used to protect a motor from too much current?

A) Magnetic or Thermal trips
B) An under-voltage relay and associated circuit breakers
C) The large impedance of the cables lowers the load current.
D) Earth and associated circuit breaker

Answer: A

Explanation: By fusing a current-sensitive electromagnetic device with a temperature-sensitive device, an MCCB offers protection.

2. _____ motor should always be started with a load

A) D.C. series motor
B) Induction motor
C) D.C. shunt motor
D) Repulsion motor

Answer: A

Explanation: Because it will revolve at a critically high speed without any load, a D.C. motor in series ought to constantly be started using a load.

3. In order to put out an electrical fire, extinguishers like carbon dioxide and dry chemicals are used:

A) False
B) True

Answer: B

4. A fused switch's fuse connections are made to be _____:

A) Made stationary.
B) Separate from moving contacts.
C) Mounted on moving contacts.
D) Interchangeable

Answer: C

Explanation: When a live wire receives too much current, the fuse wire immediately melts, shielding the device from harm. Therefore, after the switch, a fuse wire is attached to the live wire.

5. Find the current flowing in the circuit when a 120V voltage source is linked to a 5-ohm electrical bulb.

A) 26 amps
B) 20 amps
C) 22 amps
D) 24 amps

Answer: D

Explanation: $V=IR$

$I=V/R=120/5=24$ amps

6. A parallel connection between a dc ammeter and a low-value resistor is known as a _____:

A) Shunt
B) Link
C) Rheostat
D) Multiplier

Answer: A

Explanation: Shunt resistance is a term used to describe a resistor with an extremely low resistance value.

7. When the supply system is linked to _____, non-sinusoidal current and voltage waveforms are produced:

A) Resistive load
B) Linear load
C) Non-linear load

Answer: C

Explanation: The load whose current-consumption characteristics differ from the voltage being applied waveform's fundamental shape is known as a non-linear load.

8. _____ switch is referred to as such if the blades are placed in such a way as to make or break each pole simultaneously.

A) Dual Switch
B) Splitter switch
C) One-way switch
D) Linked switch.

Answer: D

Explanation: The dual switch is used in residential devices and industrial and domestic electrical systems to redirect two current cables to another set of lines.

9. With a power factor of 0.75, a motor connected to 120V supply mains uses 10 amps of current. Motor's power consumption _____:

A) 900 watts
B) 1000 watts
C) 850 watts
D) 950 watts

Answer: A

Explanation: P= VI Cos θ= 120*10*0.75= 900 watts

10. When provided with incandescent bulbs, less electricity frequencies____ stress the eyes.

A) 50 H.Z.
B) 25HZ

Answer: A

Explanation: High-intensity infrared rays can harm the cornea, perhaps cause cataracts, and cause thermal damage to the retina.

Practice Test 7

1. The resistance of capacitor ____ with increased Frequency in a capacitive circuit.

A) Increase
B) Decrease
C) Remains same

Answer: B

Explanation: As the frequency of a capacitor's plates rises, the capacitor's capacitive reactance falls. Therefore, the relationship between frequency and capacitive reactance is inverse.

2. If the voltage wave in a circuit is before the current wave, the circuit has the _____ nature:

A) Inductive
B) Resistive
C) Capacitive

Answer: A

Explanation: The electrical current lags when voltage is applied by 90° in a completely inductive circuit because the supplied voltage must always be opposite and equal to the self-induced EMF.

3. Typically, in motorized controllers', magnetic switches are used.

A) True
B) False

Answer: A

4. The induction motor's torque is equal to the_____.

A) 1/((Voltage)2)
B) (Voltage)2
C) (Voltage)3
D) (Voltage)

Answer: B

Explanation: A 3-phase induction motor's torque is inversely related to rotor P.F., rotor current, and flux per stator pole.

5. ___ cable has less radius of bending and is easily turned.

A) Stranded Conductor Cable
B) Solid Conductor Cable

Answer: A

Explanation: To prevent the cable from damage, a minimum bend radius is necessary.

6. The switch utilized in the tap-changing transformer is ____.

A) Drum Switch
B) Hydraulic Switch
C) Dial Switch
D) Magnetic Switch

Answer: C

Explanation: Through a dial switch, controlling a transformer's output voltage by changing the total number of turns in a single winding is done, which also affects the transformer's turn ratio.

7. In U.F. Cable of Underground Feeder, solid-core vinyl wrapping in either white or grey is often provided _____:

A) Protection against the physical harm
B) Protection against the leakage of current
C) Protection against the water ingress
D) Confining the magnetic Flux

Answer: C

Explanation: The underground feeder cable is utilized for protection against water ingress.

8. The harmonics in the transformer results in the _____.

A) Hysteresis losses
B) Eddy Current losses
C) Both A and B

Answer: C

Explanation: Copper and Iron losses in transformers rise as a result of harmonics. Voltage distortion puts the utilized insulating material under too much stress and increases losses from eddy and hysteresis currents.

9. ___ is the symmetrical fault.

A) Double line to ground fault
B) Three phase faults
C) Single phase fault
D) Line-to-line fault

Answer: B

Explanation: A defect that affects all phases equally, such that the system maintains balance, is known as a symmetrical fault which happens in three-phase faults.

10. ___ remains the same when the circuit is in series.

A) Voltage
B) Current
C) Both A and B
D) None of above

Answer: B

Explanation: In a series connection, each resistor has the same current flowing through it.

Practice Test 8

1. Four (4) size 2 AWG THWN insulated conductors with a total length of six (6) feet are contained in a service-entrance conduit for a commercial building. The permitted ampacity of each of these conductors is _____.

A) 110 amperes
B) 92 amperes
C) 115 amperes
D) 100 amperes

Answer: B

Explanation: Given that four conductors are carrying the current in the raceway in this case, the appropriate correction factor (derating value) from Table 310.15(B) (3)(a) must be used as follows:

Before derating: 2 AWG THWN ampacity = 115 amperes

80 percent of 115 amperes equals 92 amperes.

2. The use of conductors in damp environments is NOT permitted if they have the marking _____ on the insulation.

A) THWN
B) THHN
C) THW
D) THHW

Answer: B

Explanation: THHN-insulated conductors are only permitted for use in dry and damp places, but THWN, THHW, and THW-insulated conductors are acceptable for use in dry and wet situations, as specified in Table 310.104(A).

3. The NEC states that fixed outside snow melting and de-icing equipment should be considered a _____ load.

A) Simultaneous
B) Non-continuous
C) Continuous
D) Intermittent

Answer: C

Explanation: A continuous load is anticipated to last for three (3) hours or longer.

4. The local utility company provides a 120/240 volt, single-phase electrical system for a one-family residence with a demand load of 200 amperes. What size aluminum THW conductors are MINIMUMLY needed for this home's service entrance conductors?

A) 2/0 AWG
B) 1/0 AWG
C) 3/0 AWG
D) 4/0 AWG

Answer: D

Explanation: Aluminium conductors of size 4/0 AWG THW with a permissible ampacity of 180 amperes should be used for this residence, according to Table 310.15(B)(16).

5. The cable _____ when installing non-metallic sheathed cable encased in a submerged PVC conduit.

A) Is prohibited
B) Must be Type NMC
C) Must be Type NMW
D) Must be Type NMS

Answer: A

Explanation: In Part II of Article 334, limitations on non-metallic encased cables are covered. Type NMC is allowed in dry, moist, and damp environments, according to Section 334.10(B) (1). However, wet locations are not mentioned in this list. Types of NM and NMS cables cannot be put in moist or damp places, according to Section 334.12(B) (4).

6. The full-load current rating, expressed in amperes, of the secondary of a 150 kVA, single-phase transformer with a secondary voltage of 120/240 is _____.

A) 1250 amperes
B) 625 amperes
C) 526 amperes
D) 265 amperes

Answer: B

Explanation: Apply the single-phase current calculation as shown to determine the single-phase transformer's full-load current rating:

I = 15,000/240 = 625 amperes (150 kVA times 1000)

7. What is the highest allowable length of the 200-ampere busway where protection from overcurrent is not given when a 200-amp rated busway is tapped from a 600-amp valued busway, and solely in establishing the industry?

A) 125 feet
B) 100 feet
C) 75 feet
D) 50 feet

Answer: D

Explanation: If the busway with the smaller ampacity is no longer than fifty (50) feet in length and has an ampacity of at least one-third higher than the rating of the larger way's overcurrent protection, then overcurrent protection is not necessary at the point where the busway size is changed for busways only in industrial establishments.

8. What circuit breaker on the list below DOESN'T have a standard rating in ampere?

A) 225 amperes
B) 75 amperes
C) 110 amperes
D) 90 amperes

Answer: B

Explanation: It is not a typical ampere rating for a circuit breaker to have a 75-ampere rating.

9. The maximum allowed cord-and-plug-attached load to the receptacle is _____ when a 15-ampere 125-volt, receptacle is linked to a branch circuit of 120 volts supplying more than two receptacles or outlets.

A) 7.5 amperes
B) 12 amperes
C) 10 amperes
D) 15 amperes

Answer: B

Explanation: Under these circumstances, a 15-ampere rated receptacle can handle a maximum cord-and-plug-connected load of 12 amps.

10. For the purpose of splicing conductors or connecting to luminaires or devices, the minimum length of free conductors that must be left at each junction box is ____.

A) 6 inches
B) 4 inches
C) 8 inches
D) 10 inches

Answer: A

Explanation: Each junction box must have at least 6 inches of open conductor available for splices or the connecting of luminaires or other devices.

Practice Test 9

1. By the NEC, whether a general-use receptacle, lighting parts, or other appliances are supplied from the branch circuit, the rating of a 120V, cord-and-plug-connected air conditioner shall not be greater than _____ of the rating of the branch circuit.

A) 80%
B) 40%
C) 70%
D) 50%

Answer: D

Explanation: The overall rating of the air conditioner must not exceed 50%, which also supplies lighting units, general-use receptacles, or appliances to avoid overloading the circuit.

2. The pipes of metal water must be bonded to _____ before being put in or attached to a building or structure.

A) The service equipment enclosure.
B) The grounding electrode conductor.
C) The grounded conductor at the service.
D) Any of the above options.

Answer: D

Explanation: It is recommended to have shielding of the cable if it is within six ft. of the closer edge of the attic entry or scuttle hole.

3. _____ should not be placed over the stairway?

A) Junction boxes
B) General-use receptacles
C) Switches controlling luminaires
D) Overcurrent devices

Answer: D

Explanation: "The overcurrent gadgets shall not be positioned oversteps of a stairway." This requirement deals with a significant safety concern.

4. A minimum of one (1) single-phase, 125-volt, 15- or 20-ampere receptacle must be placed not greater than _____ and not lower than _____ from and from the inside wall of any outdoor swimming pool that is permanently erected on residential or commercial property.

A) 5 feet, 20 feet
B) 6 feet, 20 feet
C) 6 feet, 6 inches, 10 feet
D) 10 feet, 20 feet

Answer: B

Explanation: Each permanently installed swimming pool must have at least one (1) single-phase, 15- or 20-ampere, 125-volt outlet that is positioned between six and twenty feet away from the pool.

5. Suppose all the lights are connected in parallel; now one light is turned off; what is the effect on circuit resistance?

A) Resistance remains same
B) Increase
C) Decrease

Answer: B

Explanation: Because voltage is inversely proportional to resistance so, by decreasing voltage, resistance increase.

6. The magnitude of the GFCI tools which are utilized to predict the grounding fault is as low as _____:

A) 1 mA
B) 100 mA
C) 5 mA
D) 500 mA

Answer: C

Explanation: Even at current levels as low as 4 or 5 milliamps, the GFCI will detect the difference between the electricity coming into the circuit and that flowing out.

7. In a system, reactive power is necessary to maintain _____.

A) Frequency
B) Voltage
C) Both A and B

Answer: B

Explanation: It is possible to regulate reactive power production to preserve constant terminal voltage by using a voltage regulator.

8. The material of Dielectric often consists of:

A) Semiconductor
B) Insulating material
C) Conductor

Answer: B

Explanation: In the dielectric, the substance is composed of atoms. A positive terminal charge at the center of each atom is surrounded and bonded by a cloud of electrons with a negative charge.

9. Which of the following supply frequencies is preferable for voltage regulation:

A) 25 H.Z.
B) 50 H.Z.
C) 10 H.Z.
D) 12 H.Z.

Answer: B

Explanation: The source voltage is 230 V, and the frequency of the electrical transmission is 50 Hz.

10. The fault resistance is higher in the fault known as _____.

A) Bolted Fault
B) Arc Fault
C) Both A and B
D) None of the above

Answer: B

Explanation: While an arcing fault current has an impedance connected to the arc, a bolted fault has no connection to the impedance.

Practice Test 10

1. A 125-volt, 15- or 20-ampere receptacle for in-sink garbage disposal installed under the counter in a housing unit needs _____.

A) AFCI protection only
B) GFCI protection only
C) Both AFCI and GFCI protection
D) Neither GFCI nor AFCI protection

Answer: C

Explanation: Any 15- or 20-ampere 125-volt connector built within six (6) feet of a sink must be GFCI protected) because the wet surfaces increase the risk of an electric shock. All 120-volt, 15- or 20-ampere branch circuits that supply outlets in homes' kitchens must have AFCI protection.

2. Conductors for overhead service drops should generally not be less than.

A) 8 AWG copper
B) 2 AWG copper
C) 6 AWG copper
D) 4 AWG copper

Answer: A

Explanation: Overhead service-drop conductors should be no smaller than 8 AWG copper, 6 AWG aluminum, or copper-clad aluminum. Do not mistake service-entrance conductors from the utility company's service point for the service disconnecting mechanism with service-drop conductors. These overhead conductors link the utilities' electric supply system and the service point.

3. If ground-fault protection is absent, the meter enclosure is grounded to the _____ conductor. Which is on the service disconnect load side in a building or where the meter enclosure is close to the service disconnecting mechanism.

A) Phase
B) Grounded
C) Bonding
D) Grounding

Answer: B

Explanation: The meter enclosure may be grounded via a connection on the load side of the service disconnect.

4. All single-phase, 15- and 20-ampere 125-volt receptacles located within six ft. of the top inner edge of the washbasin bowl in _____ must be protected by a GFCI in residential units.

A) Laundry rooms
B) Garages
C) Bathrooms
D) All of the above

Answer: D

Explanation: GFCI protection must be installed to prevent a ground-fault shock hazard regardless of the location or room in the house where the 15- or 20-ampere, 125-volt receptacles are positioned within six (6) feet of the top inside edge of the washbasin bowl.

5. Why is metallic conduit required to have electrical continuity?

A) To reduce electrolysis.
B) To reduce voltage drop.
C) To establish an effective ground-fault path and facilitate the operation of the overcurrent protective device.
D) To limit galvanic corrosion.

Answer: C

Explanation: Metallic conduit must have electrical continuity to create a reliable ground-fault channel and make the overcurrent protective device work more efficiently.

6. P.V. source circuits within the P.V. array may use cable having single-conductor like _____ and such cables are classified and known to be solar photovoltaic (P.V.) wire.

A) PVC-2
B) UF
C) USE-2
D) THHN

Answer: C

Explanation: Open, single-conductors, like single-conductor and Type USE-2 cable labeled and recognized as P.V. wire, are allowed to be used in P.V. supply circuits inside the P.V. array.

7. When installed in residential units, receptacle outlets for countertop surfaces must be placed above the countertop or work surface, but not more than _____ above it.

A) 12 inches
B) 24 inches
C) 20 inches
D) 18 inches

Answer: C

Explanation: Receptacle ports built for countertops or surfaces for work in dwelling units may be placed on or above, but not higher than 20 inches above, the countertop or work surface. The purpose of this regulation is to prohibit the placement of unattractive cables for an extension on the countertop or work surface to supply cord-and-plug linked appliances (which decreases the amount of available countertop space). Additionally, outlets placed more than 20 inches above counters or work surfaces may obstruct cabinetry installation.

8. The manually operated switch for the emergency lighting systems can often be placed anywhere in a movie theatre.

A) In the motion picture projection booth
B) On the stage or platform
C) In an accessible location in the lobby
D) At any of the above locations

Answer: C

Explanation: If the usual power supply fails, emergency lighting systems are built and designed to provide a certain illumination level for exits from the structure.

9. The ampacity modification factors for a maximum of three conductors in the raceway are not required to be used when conductors are put in a conduit or tubing nipple that is _____ or less in length.

A) 48 inches
B) 24 inches
C) 36 inches
D) 30 inches

Answer: B

Explanation: The adjustment factors for raceways with more than three (3) conductors carrying current do not apply when the racetrack is no longer than 24 inches.

The permitted ampacity of the conductors is not significantly reduced when more than three conductors carrying current are put in tubing with short lengths since the supplementary conductors have a negligible heating effect.

GLOSSARY OF TERMINOLOGY

NAME	DEFINITION
Atom	The smallest amount of substance that can be separated without releasing electrically charged particles.
Block diagram	A block diagram can be used to graphically illustrate a system and provides a functional description of the system.
Bonding	It is connected to provide continuity and electrical conductivity.
Bonding Conductor	It is a reliable conductor that ensures the essential conductivity of electricity required for metal-to-metal connections.
Circuit diagram	It is a typical graphical representation of a circuit that has been simplified.
Closed-loop control system	A closed-loop control system is an electrical or mechanical gadget that constantly adjusts a system to maintain a desirable condition or set point without requiring the interaction of humans.
Control system	A control system is made up of several mechanical or electrical parts that work together to regulate other parts or systems using control loops.
Current	Current is the flow of charge carriers.
Electric Charge	Subatomic particles exert a force when they are in an electric and magnetic field because of their electric charge.
Electric Motors	A tool that transforms electrical energy into mechanical energy is an electric motor.
Electric Power	Electric power is the amount of electrical energy that is lost or consumed within an electric circuit.
Electrical Box	It is used to protect connections for various reasons, like switches and electrical outlets, from outside loss, alteration, and other components that could affect their functioning.

Electrical drawing	Electrical drawings, sometimes called wiring diagrams, are technical drawings that provide visual explanations of electrical systems or circuits.
Electrical Network	An electrical network is made up of many circuit parts and EMF sources connected.
Electrical Raceways	It is an electrical wire channel made by a physically reachable conduit. Raceways provide physical protection for wires and cables from hazards such as warmth, water intrusion, moisture, corrosion, and erosion.
Electrical Wiring	An outlet, light fixture, appliance, device, socket, cable, distribution board cable, or switch uses an electrical wire to transfer power from a transformer and other sources of electricity.
Electricity	Electricity is the movement of electrical power.
Equipment Bonding Jumper	It is used for connecting more than one piece of grounding conductor inside the equipment.
Feeder	In power networks, feeders are the power cables used to carry electricity. Power is delivered to distribution locations via a feeder from a producing station or substation.
Grounding	Connected to the earth or a conductive object that extends the ground connection.
KCL	The total number of currents flowing into and out of a junction in an electrical circuit is equal.
KVL	Voltage differences in any closed loop equal algebraically to zero.
Lighting system	Plants, devices, and other objects used or helpful in the system's supply of resources and accessories, including lighting.
Line Diagram	A single-line diagram, often known as an SLD or one-line diagram, is a straightforward representation of an electrical system.
Main Bonding Jumper	It is the connection at the service between the bonding jumper on the supply side and the grounding conductor of the equipment, or both, and the grounded circuit conductor.
Ohm's Law	An electrical law states that the current flowing through a circuit is equal to its resistance divided by its potential difference.
Open-loop control system	It is a type of control where the output relies on the input but is unrelated to the controller or input.
Pictorial Diagram	A diagram that represents the parts of a system using realistic photos or abstract graphic designs.

Solidly-Grounding	It was linked to the ground when no resistor or other impedance-reducing component was present.
Step-down Transformer	To reduce AC voltage or AC sources, a type of transformer known as a step-down transformer is utilized.
Step-up Transformer	To convert low-voltage current into high-voltage current, step-up transformers are employed.
Switch	A device for making, breaking, or changing connections inside an electrical circuit.
Transformer	Altering the voltage of alternating current is the function of an inductive electrical transformer.
Voltage	The force required to move an electric charge along an electric circuit from one point to another is expressed in voltage.
Wiring Diagram	In a wiring diagram, the actual location of the parts and the wire connections are depicted.

CONCLUSION

The Journeyman Electrician Exam Prep manual is a priceless tool for electricians who want to succeed. Aspiring journeyman electricians can use this comprehensive guide's wide range of knowledge to help them navigate the complicated and always-changing world of electrical work. Electricians are given an in-depth knowledge of electrical theory, codes, laws, and real-world applications throughout the guide. Electrical circuits, wiring systems, electrical equipment, safety procedures, and troubleshooting methods are only a few subjects covered in the guide. Electricians who have completely studied and mastered these ideas can take the journeyman electrician exam with assurance, knowing they have the know-how to succeed.

The manual also helps practice questions and simulated tests that replicate the real exam structure and degree of difficulty. This enables electricians to evaluate their knowledge and pinpoint their areas of development, allowing them to strategically direct their study efforts. Each question has comprehensive explanations and solutions, ensuring that electricians not only learn from their errors but also have a better comprehension of the guiding ideas.

Beyond exam studying, electricians can use this book as a reference throughout their careers. Electrical contractors can take on challenging electrical projects with assurance and precision thanks to the quantity of information offered, along with relevant examples and pictures. Throughout their careers, it supports them in staying current with the most recent industry standards and best practices by acting as dependable friends.

Ultimately, the Journeyman Electrician Exam Prep book equips electricians with the knowledge, abilities, and success they need to advance in their chosen fields. It is a thorough, well-organized, and essential resource that gives electricians the knowledge and assurance necessary to become licensed journeymen electricians.

Made in the USA
Monee, IL
16 August 2023

41116014R00083